World Cultures Past and Present

Teacher's Guide

Level F

ISBN 0-8172-6561-9

STECK-VAUGHN
COMPANY
ELEMENTARY • SECONDARY • ADULT • LIBRARY

ACKNOWLEDGMENTS

Executive Editor: Diane Sharpe

Project Editor: Janet Jerzycki

Assistant Art Director: Cynthia Ellis

Design Manager: John J. Harrison

Program Development, Design, Illustration,
and Production: Proof Positive/Farrowlyne Associates, Inc.

Contents

The Philosophy of Steck-Vaughn Social Studies

Social studies focuses on developing knowledge and skill in history, geography, anthropology, economics, and political science. Most importantly, it focuses on people and their interaction with each other and the world in which they live. *Steck-Vaughn Social Studies* addresses these areas of study in a six-level program that correlates with the social studies curriculum throughout the United States. This program can serve as an alternative to traditional basal textbooks. *Steck-Vaughn Social Studies* helps students acquire the skills, knowledge, and understanding they must have in order to function as concerned and involved members of our society.

Steck-Vaughn Social Studies is a program that both you and your students will enjoy using. Its approach is based on widening the horizons of students as they progress through the elementary grades. Students will gain a concrete, understandable framework for learning the principles of democracy and citizenship. They will also gain a better vantage point from which to view the world's diversity.

ABOUT THE PUPIL EDITIONS

The individual features of *Steck-Vaughn Social Studies* have been designed to help students meet with success in their study of social studies. A variety of features work together to create books that are both inviting and manageable for students who have difficulty reading in this content area.

Format

The pupil texts are divided into units and chapters of manageable length. Each unit opener identifies the important concepts of the unit and sets the stage for successful reading by asking questions to spark student interest. A photograph welcomes students to each new unit. The unit opener also suggests an idea for an appealing cooperative learning project for students to carry out as they read the unit. The unit closes with suggestions of ways students can complete and present their project.

Interactive Activities

Activities on the pupil edition pages ensure student involvement by asking them to respond to the text. Many of the activities emphasize geography skills. Activities also include recall questions, higher-level thinking questions, and activities that require student interaction with maps, charts, and illustrations.

Readability

A readable and manageable text draws students into the content and ensures their understanding. The text never talks down to students or overwhelms them, but rather respects them and presents the content in a form they will understand and enjoy. Difficult concepts are presented in a straightforward manner. The students' prior knowledge is used as a starting point for presenting new concepts. The reading level is carefully controlled at or below grade level in order to ease the difficulties students often have with reading content-area materials.

Text	Reading Level
Level A	Grade 1
Level B	Grade 2
Level C	Grade 2
Level D	Grade 3
Level E	Grade 3
Level F	Grade 4

Vocabulary

Key social studies terms are boldfaced and defined in context in the texts. The glossary at the end of each book lists the terms and their definitions alphabetically.

Special Feature Pages

These pages appear at the end of every chapter and focus on a person, place, or event that extends the chapter content. For example, "Around the Globe" special features in Level C take students to Australia and Canada. In the chapter about ancient Egypt in Level F, the "Special People" feature focuses on Hatshepsut. One "For Your Information" in Level E extends the content of the Civil War with a description of the Freedmen's Bureau set up to help African Americans after the war.

History Strand

Steck-Vaughn Social Studies addresses the often neglected need for history in the lower grades. For example, students at Level A read about the first families in the United States—American Indians and Pilgrims. At Level C, students explore the development of a community—Omaha, Nebraska—from the days of the Omaha people to the present.

Skills Program

Each unit includes social studies and geography skills such as maps, globes, charts, and graphs as part of its narrative content. A Skill Builder at the end of each unit extends the content, at the same time reviewing a social studies or geography skill taught previously in the unit.

Maps and Illustrations

Students are drawn into the texts by abundant maps and illustrations that enhance their understanding of the content.

Chapter Checkups

Checkup tests provide successful closure to each chapter. The consistent format helps students feel comfortable in a review situation. Each Checkup consists of questions in standardized test format, which address the factual content of the chapter. A critical-thinking-and-writing question that requires students to display their deeper understanding of a chapter concept concludes the chapter.

ABOUT THE TEACHER'S GUIDE

The separate Teacher's Guide presents strategies for units and chapters with guidelines and answers for the interactive text; midterm and final tests; letters to families; and useful graphic organizers.

Teaching Strategies

The unit strategies include a unit summary, pre- and post-reading activities, guidelines for implementing the unit project, and bibliographies for both teacher and student. In addition, references to the Teacher's Resource Binder blacklines are included, should you choose to purchase this additional resource.

The chapter strategies include activities for pre- and post-reading, as well as a chapter summary, objectives, a list of vocabulary along with vocabulary activities, and page-by-page teaching suggestions and answers to interactive text.

These activities can help teachers accommodate the individual and group needs of students.

Letters to Families

Family letters are provided for every unit of Levels A, B, C, and D, and for each book of Levels E and F. The letters invite families to participate in their child's study of the book and provide suggestions for some specific activities that can extend the concepts. A separate Spanish version of each letter is also provided.

Assessment and Evaluation

A mid-term and final test are provided in the Teacher's Guide for Levels C, D, E, and F. The tests are in the standardized test format familiar to students from the Chapter Checkups.

To implement portfolio assessment, invite students to select samples of their best work to supply for their portfolios. Ask them to tell you which work they are most proud of and why. You may want to suggest that students' work on the cooperative learning unit projects be considered for their portfolios. Allow students to discuss with you any work they would like to change and how they would change it.

CONTENT SCOPE AND SEQUENCE

	LEVEL A	LEVEL B	LEVEL C
HISTORY	• People, families, and neighborhoods change over time. • American Indians were the first Americans. American Indians helped the Pilgrims to survive. • National holidays and patriotic symbols remind us of our heritage.	• American Indians were the first Americans. • Christopher Columbus came to America in search of new trade routes. • American Indians helped the Pilgrims survive in America. • Neighborhoods change over time. • Holidays commemorate special events and people from our history.	• American Indians made up our nation's earliest communities. • Pioneers settled on American Indian land and built communities such as Omaha, Nebraska. • Thanksgiving celebrates an event in American history. • Each community has its own history that we can research.
GEOGRAPHY	• Families live in homes of different sizes and shapes. • Different families need or want to live in different places (near rivers, mountains, etc.). • A globe is a model of Earth. • Earth provides us with many resources.	• Neighborhoods are real places we can show on maps. • Globes are ways of showing the whole, round Earth. • Neighborhoods around the world are both alike and different. • There are seven continents on Earth. • Earth has different geographic features such as mountains, plains, rivers, and oceans.	• Life in communities often depends on natural resources, climate, and landforms. • Water is a very valuable natural resource. • Plains and mountains are important landforms. • The American Indian way of life was shaped by the land.
GOVERNMENT/ CITIZENSHIP	• Rules help us to live, work, and play at home and in the community. • We have responsibilities in our families. • Families share feelings about their country and about their flag. • It is important to take care of the environment. • Families remember great Americans and events on special days.	• We live in the United States of America. • Neighbors work together to solve mutual problems. • Rules and laws tell us what to do and what not to do. Rules and laws help us live together. • Groups have leaders (mayor, governor, President).	• A community is run by a government. • Government leaders are elected by the people of a community. • Communities have laws to tell people what to do and how to act, to protect people, and to provide safety. • Our national government is based in Washington, D.C.
ECONOMICS	• People work to earn money to buy the things they need and want. • Some people produce goods and others provide services. • We can't always have everything we want. People make choices as to which needs and wants they will satisfy.	• Some people produce goods and others provide services. • Workers cooperate to produce goods. • People use the money they earn to buy the things they need and want. • The choice of jobs may be limited by the place in which a person lives. • Taxes help pay for many community services.	• As workers, people are producers; as buyers, they are consumers. • One product may be produced by many people working in different communities. • Communities depend on one another. • Jobs and industry determine whether or not a community will grow or shrink.
SOCIOLOGY/ ANTHROPOLOGY	• Families vary in size and structure. • Families provide for physical and emotional needs and wants. Different families have somewhat different rules and private holidays. • Schools are special places for learning. • All family members can help the family meet its needs and wants.	• Neighborhoods are places in which to live, work, and play. • Neighbors vary in age, language, and other human characteristics. • People share the customs of their homelands with new friends and neighbors in the United States. • Neighbors share local and national holidays.	• Communities vary in size: rural towns, suburbs, and cities. • People live, work, and play in communities. • Living in communities makes it easier to get things done and to help people. • We have American traditions. • We also have many individual family traditions.

CONTENT SCOPE AND SEQUENCE

	LEVEL D	LEVEL E	LEVEL F
HISTORY	• The American Indians were the first to settle in what is now the U.S. • The U.S. has always been a nation of immigrants. • The geography and natural features of a region affect the course of its history.	• The history of the U.S. tells how different groups built a strong nation. • U.S. history can be divided into several distinct periods. • The study of these periods shows how people and events have shaped the present. • The study of the past shows the development of important ideas.	• Civilizations in Asia, Africa, Europe, and the Americas made key contributions to human life and knowledge. • The ancient Greeks and Romans and the nations of Western Europe have influenced many nations. • Geography, trade, and technology can affect the development of a civilization.
GEOGRAPHY	• The U.S. is a large nation. It includes 50 states and Puerto Rico. • The Northeast, Southeast, North Central, Rocky Mountain, Southwest, and Pacific regions are groups of states with characteristic geographic features. • Landforms and climate influence the way people live and work.	• The U.S. has diverse landforms, climates, and natural resources. • The U.S. can be divided into several distinct regions. • The geography of the U.S. has affected the ways in which the nation was explored and settled. • U.S. geography has influenced economic activities.	• Varied land regions, climates, resources, and bodies of water are found on Earth. • People adapt differently to different natural environments. • Latitude, altitude, and ocean currents can affect climate. Climate affects cultures. • A wise use of resources is necessary for a healthy environment.
GOVERNMENT/ CITIZENSHIP	• The U.S. is a democracy in which voters are free to choose their leaders in local, state, and national governments. • Each level of government handles different kinds of problems and functions. • Americans share pride in a heritage they have built together.	• The U.S. is a democracy. • The U.S. Constitution contains the beliefs of the colonists about freedom, equality, justice, and property. • It establishes the branches of the government. • The Constitution (including the Bill of Rights) has been the basis for the rights of Americans.	• Governments vary from dictatorships to democracies. • Ancient Greek and Roman governments influenced our own. • The roles of citizens can vary from no participation to making many political choices. • Economic upheavals and new political ideas can change government.
ECONOMICS	• Americans do many jobs that are created by the U.S.'s wealth, natural and human resources, education, and freedom to make choices as interdependent consumers and producers. • Transportation and communications systems allow the exchange of goods and materials produced in different places.	• Americans have several ways of acquiring goods, services, and property. • Natural resources and technology have influenced economic activities in different U.S. regions. • Changes in transportation and communication have affected economic activities.	• Nations trade with one another to obtain needed raw materials and goods. • Economic development is affected by a nation's government, resources, technology, trade policies, and trade practices.
SOCIOLOGY/ ANTHROPOLOGY	• Individual Americans, though diverse in occupation, family heritage, and other human characteristics, share certain American customs, languages, and symbols.	• American Indians had developed cultures before the arrival of European settlers. • Different groups have made contributions to U.S. society. • American traditions influence our approach to issues such as minority rights and conservation of resources.	• The values and beliefs of a culture influence its growth and development. • The culture of a society includes its customs and religious beliefs. • Advanced cultures have writing, art and architecture, science, and mathematics. • Trade and war can lead to the diffusion of cultures and to new cultures.

NUMBERS = PE CHAPTERS

	LEVELS:	A	B	C	D	E	F
GEOGRAPHY AND OTHER SOCIAL STUDIES SKILLS	Understanding globes	8	4	8	14		2, 12, 18
	Understanding time zones						1, 17
	Using map keys	7	1, 4, 9	1, 2, 12	1, 4, 6, 8, 10, 12, 13	3, 4, 5, 6, 8, 10, 11, 13, 14, 16, 17	2, 4, 7, 8, 10, 14, 19, 20
	Using scale and distance			1, 2, 12	4, 5, 10, 11, 14	2, 5	6, 9, 15, 16
	Working with directions	6, 7, 8, 9, 10	1, 4, 9, 11	1, 2, 3, 4, 5, 6	1, 4, 6, 7, 8, 10, 12, 13, 15	2, 8, 9	9
	Working with landforms	8	1, 5	2, 5	1, 4, 5, 7, 8, 9, 10, 11, 12	2, 17	2, 12, 16, 17, 18
	Working with latitude and longitude						2, 12, 16
	Working with maps	7, 8, 9	1, 4, 9, 10, 11	1, 2, 3, 4, 5, 6, 10, 11, 12, 13, 14	1, 2, 4, 5, 6, 7, 8, 9, 10, 11, 12, 13, 14	1, 2, 3, 4, 5, 6, 8, 9, 10, 11, 13, 14, 16, 17	1, 2, 3, 4, 5, 6, 7, 8, 9, 10, 11, 12, 13, 14, 15, 16, 17, 18, 19, 20
	Working with graphs	6	5, 7	9, 11	2, 3, 11	11, 12, 14	15, 16
	Working with time lines		12	13	13, 15	2, 5, 6	9
	Working with charts	11	3, 9	9, 11	7	2, 4, 7	6, 10
	Working with diagrams			8, 12, 15	3, 14		
	Working with tables				6		
THEMATIC STRANDS IN SOCIAL STUDIES	Culture	1, 2, 3, 4, 5, 6, 7, 8, 9, 10, 11, 12	1, 3, 4, 5, 6, 7, 8, 9, 10, 11, 12	1, 2, 3, 4, 5, 6, 7, 8, 9, 10, 11, 12, 13, 14, 15, 16	1, 2, 3, 5, 6, 7, 9, 10, 11, 12, 13, 14, 15	1, 2, 3, 4, 5, 6, 7, 8, 9, 10, 11, 12, 13, 14, 15, 16, 17, 18	1, 2, 4, 5, 6, 7, 8, 9, 10, 11, 13, 14, 15, 16, 17, 19, 20
	Time, continuity, and change	1, 4, 6, 7, 9, 10, 11, 12	2, 3, 4, 10	1, 3, 6, 9, 12, 13, 14, 15, 16	2, 3, 5, 7, 8, 9, 10, 11, 13, 14, 15	1, 2, 3, 4, 5, 6, 7, 8, 9, 10, 11, 12, 13, 14, 15, 16, 17, 18	1, 4, 5, 6, 7, 8, 9, 10, 11, 13, 14, 15, 16, 17, 18, 19, 20
	People, places, and environments	1, 2, 3, 4, 5, 6, 7, 8, 9, 10, 11, 12	1, 2, 3, 4, 5, 6, 7, 8, 9, 10, 11	1, 2, 3, 4, 5, 6, 7, 8, 9, 10, 11, 12, 13, 14, 15, 16	1, 2, 3, 5, 6, 7, 8, 9, 10, 11, 12, 13, 14, 15	1, 2, 3, 4, 5, 6, 7, 8, 9, 10, 11, 12, 13, 14, 15, 16, 17, 18	1, 2, 3, 4, 5, 6, 7, 8, 9, 10, 11, 12, 13, 14, 15, 16, 17, 18, 19, 20
	Individual development and identity	1, 2, 3, 6, 7, 8, 9, 10, 11, 12	4, 6, 7, 8, 9, 10, 11, 12	1, 3, 4, 5, 6, 8, 9, 10, 11, 12, 13, 14, 15, 16	2, 3, 4, 7, 9, 11, 13, 14, 15	1, 3, 4, 5, 6, 7, 8, 9, 10, 11, 12, 13, 14, 15, 16, 17, 18	4, 5, 6, 7, 8, 9, 10, 11, 13, 14, 15, 16, 19, 20
	Individuals, groups, and institutions	1, 2, 3, 4, 5, 6, 7, 8, 9, 10, 11, 12	1, 2, 3, 4, 5, 6, 7, 8, 9, 10, 11, 12	1, 3, 4, 6, 7, 9, 10, 11, 12, 13, 14, 15, 16	3, 4, 5, 6, 9, 10, 11, 12, 13, 14, 15	1, 2, 3, 4, 5, 6, 7, 8, 9, 10, 11, 12, 13, 14, 15, 16, 17, 18	1, 4, 5, 6, 7, 8, 9, 10, 11, 13, 14, 15, 16, 17, 19, 20
	Power, authority, and governance	1, 2, 3, 4, 5, 6, 7, 8, 9, 12	6, 7, 8, 9, 10, 11	1, 2, 3, 7, 9, 10, 11, 12, 14, 15, 16	3, 7, 9, 11, 13, 15	3, 4, 5, 6, 7, 8, 9, 10, 11, 12, 13, 14, 15, 16, 17, 18	1, 4, 5, 6, 7, 8, 9, 10, 11, 13, 14, 15, 16, 17, 19, 20
	Production, distribution, and consumption	3, 4, 5, 8, 10, 11	3, 4, 5, 6, 7, 9	1, 3, 5, 7, 8, 12, 13, 14	5, 6, 7, 8, 9, 11, 12, 13, 15	1, 3, 4, 5, 9, 10, 11, 12, 13, 14, 15, 16, 17, 18	1, 3, 4, 5, 6, 7, 8, 10, 11, 12, 13, 14, 15, 16, 17, 19
	Science, technology, and society	1, 4, 5, 7, 9	2, 5, 7, 10	1, 4, 7, 8, 10, 13, 14	1, 7, 9, 13, 14, 15	2, 3, 10, 11, 12, 13, 14, 15, 16, 17, 18	1, 3, 4, 5, 6, 8, 9, 10, 11, 13, 14, 15, 16, 18, 20
	Global connections	2, 3, 6, 8, 9, 12	1, 3, 4, 5, 10, 11, 12	5, 6, 8, 11, 16	2, 4, 5, 6, 7, 8, 10, 12, 14, 15	1, 2, 3, 5, 6, 10, 12, 15, 16, 17, 18	1, 2, 3, 4, 6, 7, 8, 9, 10, 11, 13, 14, 16, 17, 19
	Civic ideals and practice	4, 5, 6, 7, 9, 12	4, 5, 7, 8, 9, 10, 11, 12	1, 3, 7, 8, 9, 10, 11, 12, 13, 14, 15, 16	3, 4, 7, 9, 13	3, 4, 5, 6, 7, 10, 11, 12, 15, 17, 18	3, 4, 5, 6, 8, 9, 10, 11, 15, 16

Unit Summary People have formed communities all around the world. Mountains, deserts, seas, rivers, weather, and plants all make up the natural environment people live in. The environment is different in every place people have chosen to live. The different natural environments, land regions, and climates of Earth affect people's ways of life. People use Earth's resources—both renewable and nonrenewable—as a means of survival. Conservation can help slow down the overuse of nonrenewable resources and keep the supply of renewable resources clean and unpolluted.

Before Reading the Unit Introduce the unit by asking students to describe the land, waterways, and climate in your area. Help them to see how these features relate to their own ways of life. For example, if your area is used for farming, help students to understand how the relationship between the land and the climate makes this possible.

Point out the Unit Project box to students and explain that they will work on this project as they read through the unit.

Unit Project

Setting Up the Project Divide the class into teams made up of three or four students. You might want to bring in a variety of books about climate, geography, and environment to help students work on their projects.

Students will find specific suggestions in the Project Tip sections of the chapters. Encourage them to adapt the suggestions to their own interests.

Presenting the Project One alternative possibility might be for students to keep an environment diary. A different student should be responsible each day for recording some observation about the environment, the relationship of people to Earth, the use of resources, and the role of conservation.

After Reading the Unit Invite discussion of the questions on the unit opener. Prompt discussion by asking questions such as: What are some of the major land regions of Earth? What are some of the world's renewable and nonrenewable resources?

Skill Builder

Reading a Time-Zone Map

As students read page 32, remind them that one advantage of a time-zone map is that it makes it easy to see at a glance what time it is in different parts of the world. Review this concept by asking students the time difference between New York and Phoenix. (2 hours)

Answers: 1. 8:00 P.M. **2.** two **3.** You would set it back one hour.

Bibliography

Teacher
Davis, Kenneth C. *Don't Know Much About Geography: Everything You Need to Know About the World but Never Learned.* William Morrow & Co., 1992.

Geography for Life: National Geographic Standards, 1994. NCGE, 1994.

Massachusetts Geographic Alliance. *Global Geography: Activities for Teaching the Five Themes of Geography.* Social Science Education Consortium, 1990.

Posey-Pacak, Melissa L. *Earth at Risk.* NCGE, 1991.

Student
Lambert, David. *The World's Population.* (Young Geographer Series) Thomson Learning, 1993. (Grades 4–6)

Millea, Nick. *Settlements.* (Young Geographer Series) Thomson Learning, 1993. (Grades 4–6)

Owen, Oliver. *Eco-Solution: It's In Your Hands.* Raintree Steck-Vaughn, 1993. (Grades 4–6)

Taylor, Barbara. *Weather and Climate.* (Young Discoverers Series) Raintree Steck-Vaughn, 1993. (Grades 3–4)

Wheeler, Jill. *Every Drop Counts: A Book About Water.* (Eco-Resources Series) Raintree Steck-Vaughn, 1993. (Grades 3–5)

Teacher's Resource Binder

Blackline Masters for Unit 1: Unit 1 Project Organizer, Unit 1 Review, Unit 1 Test; Activities for Chapters 1, 2, 3; Outline Maps of the World, Eastern and Western Hemispheres, Latitude and Longitude

Chapter Summary People are both the same and different all over the world. People all share the same home—the planet Earth—but there are many different ways of life around the world. Technology is rapidly influencing the way people live.

Chapter Objectives Students will learn to

- identify ways in which people differ from one another.

- identify basic needs all people share.

- identify relationships between people and the natural environment.

- interpret a time-zone map.

- understand the influence of new technology, such as the Internet.

Vocabulary

communities, p. 6	culture, p. 8
natural environment, p. 7	economy, p. 8
	government, p. 8
archaeologists, p. 7	technology, p. 9
artifacts, p. 7	communicate, p. 10

Vocabulary Activities Write the word *culture* at the center of a word web. You may want to use the Concept Web found on page 62 of this guide for this purpose. Place the words *economy* and *government* on two of the spokes. Invite volunteers to explain how the economy and the government of a country contribute to a country's culture. Add the term *artifacts* to the web. Tell students that artifacts found in the United States include tools used by American Indians, while artifacts found in Egypt include gold jewelry worn by pharoahs thousands of years ago. Ask: What do artifacts tell you about the differences among cultures? For students who have difficulty with any of the vocabulary terms, help them use the glossary to review the terms.

Before Reading the Chapter Point out to students the two kinds of maps in the chapter:

a map showing traveling time across the United States, and a world time-zone map. Review how to read information presented on a map, such as the one on page 10. Ask students about the longest trip they have taken. Where did they go and how did they travel?

Teaching Suggestions and Answers
Page 6

If you have lived in another country or culture or traveled extensively, discuss with students the cultural similarities and differences you observed. If any students have had these experiences, ask them to report on their observations. Then ask students to describe their community. Ask students to list some things people do together in your community. (Answers will vary.) **Answers to the question should include differences in skin color, clothing, and head wear.**

Page 7

Discuss with students the impact of pollution on the environment. Explain how air pollution and oil spills can harm the plants and animals that are found in a place. Ask: Why would weather and the presence of animals help people decide whether they want to live in a certain place? (An area where there is regular rainfall and mild temperatures would be good for growing crops. Some animals can be used for food.) **Students might answer for transportation or to catch fish.**

Project Tip

Help students carry out the suggestion on page 7. You may want to suggest that they think about their natural environment. Does it include rich farmland, lakes and rivers, mountains, forests, and so forth? Why might people have settled in that environment? How did the natural environment help them to make a living?

Page 8

Ask students if they would eat a lot of fish if they lived near a large body of water. (Probably yes, because people make use of the resources around them.) Point out that the photographs on page 8 show an Inuit family in Alaska and villagers in Bali, Indonesia, harvesting rice. **Students should answer that people who live in a** cold climate need warm clothing, and that people who live in a tropical climate can wear lighter clothing and can farm and fish.

Page 9

Discuss with students some other ways that technology can change the natural environment. (Lakes and rivers can be drained; roads and highways can be built through heavily forested areas.) **Answers will vary but might include: VCRs to record television shows; computers to make learning easier; the Internet to gain access to information; microwave ovens to make cooking easier and faster.**

Page 10

Ask if it is faster to travel across the country by train or by automobile. (train) What is the fastest way to travel across the United States today? (airplane) **Students should circle the amount of time shown on the map for each of the following forms of transportation: stagecoach, wagon train, train, and jet airplane.**

Page 11

Explain to students that time is figured from the Prime Meridian, which passes through the town of Greenwich, England. Point out that as you move west from Greenwich, each time zone is an hour earlier. As you move east, each time zone is one hour later. Ask how many hours difference there is between the time in Anchorage, Alaska, and Rome, Italy. (11 hours) **Students should answer 9 A.M.**

Page 12

Technology Make sure that all students understand the terms introduced in the feature. Explain to students that on the "Information Superhighway," having access to the Internet is like having access to a huge electronic library. **Students will have different answers about how using E-mail and the Internet will help them find out more about geography. However, students might use E-mail to send a message to an expert in the field or request information about some question concerning geography. They might contact a center for geographical research such as the geography department at a university. They could send a message requesting information directly to another country.**

Page 13

Chapter Checkup

You may want to work through the Chapter Checkup with students.

Answers: 1. c **2.** a **3.** b **4.** c **5.** a **6.** d
Answers will vary. Possible answers include: In order to make their lives easier and more comfortable, people might wish to build houses and heat or cool their living spaces. People have also built roads so that goods can be moved from one place to another.

After Reading the Chapter

Discuss with students the things all people in the world have in common. Review the ways in which people differ. Then have students work in groups to create a bulletin-board collage of people from cultures around the world, with labels identifying their cultures and/or countries.

Civics

Have students prepare a welcome chart or book for a newcomer to your community. Students can draw pictures to show how they use the natural environment by growing a vegetable garden or by swimming and sledding.

Art

Students can make a map of their community out of a mixture of flour, salt, and water. Have them model any nearby landforms such as mountains, hills, valleys, or plains. Then have them paint the model to indicate vegetation and bodies of water.

Writing

Have students write one or two paragraphs on the subject of "Differences I Admire." First have groups of students brainstorm lists of differences among cultures. These could be abilities, skills, or ways of doing things in other cultures. Then have each student in the group use the list to write their paragraphs.

Geography/Cultural Awareness

Have students work in groups to research holidays and other special events celebrated by cultures around the world. Then have students work on a handmade calendar, incorporating the special dates. Have students decorate the calendar with magazine pictures and drawings. Students can heighten cultural awareness and celebrate geography throughout the year.

Chapter Summary The four main types of land regions on Earth are mountains, highlands, plateaus, and plains. Earth's land regions differ because they are influenced by climate. Earth's climate has changed since the distant past; glaciers once spread over many parts of Earth, creating valleys and plains. Climate is a factor people consider when deciding where to live.

Chapter Objectives Students will learn to

- identify land regions of Earth.

- identify climate regions of Earth.

- compare a map that shows climate regions with one that shows population.

- learn about volcanoes.

Vocabulary

geography, p. 14	glaciers, p. 19
mountains, p. 14	erosion, p. 20
highlands, p. 14	precipitation, p. 21
plateaus, p. 14	volcano, p. 22
plains, p. 14	lava, p. 22
climate, p. 18	crust, p. 22
rain forests, p. 18	mantle, p. 22
deserts, p. 19	

Vocabulary Activities List all the vocabulary words on the chalkboard. Have students classify them into two categories: *Words That Tell About Earth* and *Words That Tell About What Happens on Earth*. Have them give reasons for their choices. At the end of the lesson, allow students to suggest other ways of classifying the words. Remind students who have difficulty with any of the terms that they can use the glossary.

Before Reading the Chapter Show students a globe. Ask them which geographical features they can identify, such as oceans and land, the shapes and sizes of landforms and bodies of water, and possibly mountain elevation and ocean depth. Ask students about different kinds of land regions they have seen in person, seen on television or in movies, or read about in books. Encourage them to recall features such as waterfalls, geysers, and islands.

Teaching Suggestions and Answers

Page 14

Make sure students understand that geography means more than the physical features of Earth. **Students should identify the land region as a mountain region.**

Page 15

The name *Himalayas* means "House of Snow" or "Snowy Range." Point out that some mountains are so tall they are capped with snow year-round. This is because the temperature drops as you go higher. Have students name mountain ranges in South America and in Africa. **Students should identify the photo on the left as showing a plain and the photo on the right as showing a plateau.**

Project Tip
Help students carry out the suggestion on page 15. Bring in several copies of *National Geographic* or a similar magazine. Have student teams look through the magazines for ways in which people affect the geography or environment of Earth and ways in which geography or environment affects people. Encourage teams to take notes about their observations.

Page 16

Students should put an *X* near the Patagonian Plateau in South America and the Great Central Plateau in Asia, shown on the part of the map on page 17. They should answer: the Andes and the Himalayas. Point out to students that one kind of plateau is sometimes called a "mesa," the Spanish word for "table." Some plateaus rise sharply on all four sides so they look like a table.

Page 17

Ask students to identify the continent on which the Great Lowland Plain is located. (Asia) Ask students why members of the Sioux and Comanche tribes were sometimes referred to as "Plains Indians." (They lived in the Great Central Plains region of North America.)

Students should identify the plains region in North America, shown on the part of the map on page 16, as the Great Central Plains. In identifying the land region closest to their community, students' answers will vary.

Page 18

Students should identify the five different kinds of climate found on Earth as tropical, dry, moist warm, moist cold, and arctic. You might then ask how many different kinds of climate are found in the United States. (All five, including arctic in Alaska.)

Page 19

In addition to regions in the Arctic and Antarctica, glaciers can also be found in many high mountain regions. Ask students why this might be so. (The temperature is below freezing year-round at the top of most tall mountains. Glaciers as well as snow can be found at the top.) Students should answer that moist warm and moist cold climates are found mostly above the Tropic of Cancer.

Page 20

Discuss the map on pages 18–19 with students. Have them mark with an *X* those areas where glaciers would most likely be found today. Most students will say that glaciers probably are found in Arctic regions.

Page 21

Students may need some help pronouncing the word *precipitation*. Have students locate the area on the map where they live. Ask them how many people per square mile live in their area and how much rainfall their area receives each year. (Answers will vary.) Invite them to speculate about the connection between rainfall and population in their area. Ask students how much rainfall can be found between the Equator and the Tropic of Cancer. (medium to very heavy rainfall) Students should answer that people do not usually live in regions that do not receive much rain.

Page 22

For Your Information Point out to students that the word *volcano* comes from *Vulcan,* the name the ancient Romans gave to their god of fire.

Students will probably answer that people who live near a volcano could have their homes and belongings destroyed if it erupted. An underwater volcano would not cause any significant damage.

Page 23

Chapter Checkup Make sure all students understand what the correct answers are to the numbered questions.

Answers: 1. c **2.** b **3.** a **4.** a **5.** d **6.** c
Students should answer that plains are flat and it is easier to farm and build homes on land that is flat.

After Reading the Chapter

Ask students to apply their knowledge to make estimates about the population and the annual precipitation in your area. Then have them do research to verify their estimates. Ask them about the relationship between climate and population in your area.

Geography
Divide the class into four groups and assign a land region (mountains, plateaus, highlands, or plains) to each group. Have each student find or draw a picture of that region. Then have the class make a bulletin-board display or chart of the different regions.

Writing
Have students research a volcano or an earthquake and prepare a television news report about it. First, have groups of students brainstorm a list of the characteristics of a volcano or an earthquake. Then have each student write a brief news report of two or three paragraphs to be presented on television.

Culture
Charts or bulletin-board projects could include: a collage of cultures from around the world with identifying labels or a chart that shows how transportation, work, play, and sports in a certain culture relate to climate and weather.

Chapter Summary Earth has both renewable and nonrenewable resources. Coal, oil, and natural gas are the world's main sources of energy. These resources are nonrenewable. People must learn to conserve both renewable and nonrenewable resources. Pollution is another problem that can cause great damage to Earth. All people must find ways to conserve resources and reduce pollution.

Chapter Objectives Students will learn to

- identify Earth's renewable and nonrenewable resources.
- locate major coal- and oil-producing areas on a world map.
- identify Earth's main energy resources and reasons for conserving them.
- identify causes of air and water pollution.

Vocabulary

fuel, p. 24	conservation, p. 27
resources, p. 24	pollution, p. 28
renewable resources, p. 25	chemical, p. 30
nonrenewable resources, p. 25	

Vocabulary Activities Use the Concept Web graphic organizer found on page 62 of this guide to begin two word webs: *renewable resources* and *nonrenewable resources*—things the earth made a long time ago. Ask students which web they think coal belongs in. What about plants? Tell students that as they read, they will understand how these categories are used and will be able to add more resources to each word web. Help students use the glossary for words they find difficult.

Before Reading the Chapter Encourage students to talk about books they have read or television programs or movies they have seen in which spaceships traveled on long journeys. Then ask students what the people on the spaceships needed on board in order to survive. Ask students to think about what they did this morning when they were getting ready for school. What forms of power or natural resources did they use? Electricity, gasoline, coal, oil, water? Have students tell what they know about the source of each resource they name.

Teaching Suggestions and Answers

Page 24

Discuss with students some of the activities they enjoy every day, such as watching television or using a computer. Ask them what resource these activities use. (electricity) Explain that oil and coal are used to make electricity. **Students should answer that oil helps us to travel long distances because it is made into gas, which is used as fuel in cars, trucks, buses, and airplanes.**

Page 25

Discuss the map on this page with students. Then ask them which country has the most offshore oil wells. (the United States) Ask why it is important for a country to have oil and coal resources. (A country that has oil and coal resources can produce energy for businesses and homes.) **Students should circle the offshore oil wells on the map. They might name North America, Africa, Europe, Asia, or Australia.**

Page 26

Ask students why it is important to plant new trees in areas where older trees have been cut down. (New trees must be planted if lumber is to remain a renewable resource.) Ask students to name the kinds of resources available in the area where they live. **Students should answer that lumber is a renewable resource because when a tree is cut down, another one can be planted to take its place.**

Project Tip

Help students carry out the suggestion on page 26. Suggest that they think about nonrenewable resources in their region. Are there other available resources they might substitute for nonrenewable resources? Is it possible that technology might develop substitutes for the nonrenewable resources we use today?

Page 27

Point out to students that many scientists believe that all life would be threatened if the rain forests in the Amazon were destroyed. The rain forests produce up to 60 percent of the world's oxygen; if it disappeared, air quality throughout the world would be affected. **Answers will vary.**

Page 28

Ask students to explain why air pollution is a greater problem in a city than in the country. (A city has more automobiles; therefore, pollution is more of a problem in the city.) Discuss with students the impact of pollution on the environment. Use the Cause and Effect graphic organizer on page 64 of this guide to illustrate how air pollution and oil spills can harm plants and animals. Invite students to think of other causes of pollution and the effect these pollutants have on the environment. Record students' ideas on the Cause and Effect graphic organizer. **Answers will vary.**

Page 29

Ask students to offer suggestions on what people, companies, and countries can do to help prevent oil spills in the future. **Students should circle the lighter areas in the water, which signal pollution.**

Page 30

Special People Ask students what this kind of story is called. (biography) Explain to students that DDT and other pesticides are capable of contaminating human food supplies because people may eat plants or animals that have been exposed to the chemical. Tell students that DDT was banned in the United States in 1972. **Answers will vary. Students might suggest driving less and stopping the use of harmful chemicals.**

Page 31

Chapter Checkup You may want to work through the Chapter Checkup with students.

Answers: 1. b **2.** a **3.** c **4.** b **5.** a **6.** d
The problems of pollution are becoming clearer to more people. People know that they cannot live safe, healthy lives if they continue to pollute and destroy the environment.

After Reading the Chapter

Review with students the difference between renewable and nonrenewable resources. Discuss what students can do to conserve resources that they use.

Ecology
Have students make antipollution posters for your school or community. Supplement the project with a guest speaker from a local environmental or conservation group.

Drama
Divide the class into groups to play a version of the "Desert Island" game. Tell them that they are going to take a long trip on a spaceship and that they will have everything they will need to survive in outer space. They can also take five special things with them—either food, books, or other personal items. What would they take, and why? Invite several groups to enact a short scenario showing what the group chose and why they made the decisions they did.

Writing
Have students write a poem about Earth's resources, with a different stanza for each resource. They can write the poem as light verse, using rhyme if they choose.

Geography
Suggest that students choose the one land region where they would most like to live. Have them explain in an oral report why they would choose that land region.

Ecology
Ask students to find out about recycling in your community. Students who participate in newspaper drives or other recycling activities can report to the class.

Unit Summary Civilization developed in steps that included domesticating animals, building permanent homes, developing technology and trade, making intellectual achievements, and creating laws. These steps developed in ancient times in the Fertile Crescent, Egypt, India, China, and Africa. Each of these civilizations made important contributions to future cultures.

Before Reading the Unit Introduce the unit by showing students the Fertile Crescent, Egypt, India, China, and Africa on a map or globe.

Have students open their books to the unit opener on page 34. Discuss with students the study of history and why it is important. Have them tell what kinds of things they can learn from history. Encourage students to think about the questions as they read the unit.

Point out the Unit Project box to students and explain that they will work on this project as they read through the unit.

Unit Project

Setting Up the Project Before students start the project, you might want to elaborate on the kind of work archaeologists do. Explain to students that there are three types of archaeological evidence. 1. *Artifacts* are objects that were made by people, such as arrowheads, pottery, and jewelry. 2. *Features* are another thing archaeologists study. Houses, tombs, canals, and other large structures people built fall into this category. 3. *Ecofacts* are a third type of evidence. Ecofacts are natural items that reveal how an ancient people interacted with their environment. Seeds and animal bones are ecofacts.

Students will find specific suggestions in the Project Tip sections of the chapters. Encourage them to adapt these suggestions to their own interests.

Presenting the Project One alternative possibility might be for students to make a catalogue of their museum display. The catalogue would include drawings or pictures of the artifacts they have collected and brief descriptions of the items. The catalogue might be used by visitors to the museum display. Students might invite another class to visit their museum display. They could include a copy of the catalogue with an invitation to the other class.

After Reading the Unit Invite discussion of the questions on the unit opener and the answers students discovered about ancient civilizations. Ask: What were some of the major ancient civilizations? What contributions did these civilizations make to human development? What do these civilizations have in common with one another? In what ways do they differ?

Skill Builder

Comparing Distance Scales

As students read page 67, remind them that distance scales are useful because they enable us to measure the distance between two points on a map. Point out that the distance scale is not the same on all maps. Ask students to explain the reason for this.

Answers: 1. about 400 miles **2.** inset map; about 110 kilometers **3.** about 120 miles on both maps.

Bibliography

Teacher

Demko, G. *Why in the World: Adventures in Geography.* Doubleday/Anchor, 1992.

Hull, Robert. *African Stories.* (Tales from Around the World Series) Thomson Learning, 1994. (Grades 5–6)

Student

Burns, Peggy, and Julian Rowe. *Language and Writing.* (Legacies Series) Thomson Learning, 1995. (Grades 4–5)

Clayton, Peter A. *The Valley of the Kings.* (Digging Up the Past Series) Thomson Learning, 1996. (Grades 5–6)

Coote, Roger. *The Egyptians.* (Look into the Past Series) Thomson Learning, 1993. (Grades 4–6)

Waterlow, Julia. *The Ancient Chinese.* (Look into the Past Series) Thomson Learning, 1994. (Grades 4–6)

Wood, Richard. *Architecture.* (Legacies Series) Thomson Learning, 1995. (Grades 4–5)

Teacher's Resource Binder

Blackline Masters for Unit 2: Unit 2 Project Organizer, Unit 2 Review, Unit 2 Test; Activities for Chapters 4, 5, 6, 7; Outline Maps of the World, Africa, Asia

Chapter Summary The land of Mesopotamia, known as the Fertile Crescent, was the site of a number of early civilizations. The people of Sumer created the first civilization in Mesopotamia about 5,000 years ago. The Hebrew people also had their beginnings in the Fertile Crescent.

Chapter Objectives Students will learn to

- identify the signs that indicate that a civilization has developed.

- differentiate among the Sumerian, Babylonian, and Hebrew cultures.

- identify the origins and the importance of laws that govern society.

- locate Mesopotamia (including the Tigris and Euphrates rivers and Babylon) and Canaan on a map.

Vocabulary	
civilization, p. 35	conquered, p. 38
fertile, p. 36	drought, p. 39
domesticate, p. 36	slaves, p. 39
cuneiform, p. 37	monotheism, p. 40
irrigate, p. 38	Judaism, p. 40
temple, p. 38	Exodus, p. 40
ziggurat, p. 38	

Vocabulary Activities Write the vocabulary words on the chalkboard. Then have students look at the cuneiform tablet on page 37 of the textbook. Explain that *cuneiform* was a system of writing invented by the Sumerians. Have students work in small groups to find other illustrations in the chapter that relate to the vocabulary terms. Direct students who have difficulty with any of the terms to use the glossary.

Before Reading the Chapter Ask students to discuss the difference between domesticated animals and wild animals. Discuss with them the different jobs that domesticated animals do for

people. Ask them how and why they think animals were first domesticated.

Remind students that many thousands of years ago, people did not have alphabets. Ask them to suggest some reasons why people may have developed the first writing systems.

Tell students that in early human history, people lived in small groups. They hunted animals and gathered plants to eat. Ask students to think about why people might eventually have chosen to form small communities and towns.

Teaching Suggestions and Answers
Page 35

The word *Mesopotamia* comes from a Greek word that means "land between the rivers." Ask students why this is a good word to describe the civilization that began there. (The civilization began in the river valley formed by two rivers, the Tigris and the Euphrates.) **Students might suggest that in modern cities buildings are taller and there are cars.**

Page 36

Have students look at the map on this page. Ask them what large body of water the Tigris and Euphrates rivers empty into. (the Persian Gulf) Then, discuss the disadvantages of having to move from place to place looking for food. **Students should answer that Nineveh, Babylon, Lagash, and Ur were near the Tigris and Euphrates rivers.**

Page 37

Point out to students that the word *cuneiform* comes from the Latin word *cuneus*, meaning "wedge." Cuneiform characters are shaped like a wedge, or triangle-shaped, because Sumerian writers used a wedge-shaped tool to make the characters. Ask students why people would build their homes near other people. What advantages does being in a community have for people? (People who live near each other can help each other to farm and to build things. They can also trade with each other.) **Students should answer that in addition to keeping records and lists, people can use writing to create stories and to communicate with others.**

Project Tip

Help students carry out the suggestion on page 37. Suggest that students make a list of the various kinds of artifacts that archaeologists might dig up in their excavations. They can consult this list in making their museum display.

Page 38

Point out that a canal is a waterway that is dug across land. People in early times often dug canals to connect their fields with a nearby river. Discuss what made Mesopotamia such a good place for civilizations to develop. Discuss with students whether they think the main idea behind Hammurabi's laws is a good one. **Students should answer that Babylon is northwest of Ur in Sumer.**

Page 39

Point out that Abraham lived in the city of Ur in Sumer. The Sumerians believed in many gods, but Abraham believed in only one God. According to the Bible, Abraham left Ur at God's command and went to a land called Canaan. God told Abraham that Canaan would belong to him and the people who came after him. **Students should answer that the Hebrews left Canaan because of a drought.**

Page 40

Ask students if they have ever heard of the Golden Rule: "Do unto others as you would have them do unto you." Discuss with them how this rule is similar to other rules about behavior. Discuss why laws are important for a community. **Students should indicate that modern laws against stealing, killing, and other actions are similar to actions forbidden by the Ten Commandments.**

Page 41

Special People Ask students what made Moses such a good leader. (He was brave and led his people to freedom.) Explain to students that the statue of Moses in the picture on this page was made by an Italian artist named Michelangelo in the year 1513. Tell them that they will read about Michelangelo later in this book. **Students should answer that the Hebrews needed laws to help them keep order and to live together peacefully in a new land.**

Page 42

Chapter Checkup You may want to work through the Chapter Checkup with students.

Answers: 1. c **2.** b **3.** d **4.** a **5.** a **6.** d Students might answer that without a written language, there is no way that people can keep records. These records might include amounts of goods traded, land surveys, and city activities. In addition, without written language there would not be a way to accurately preserve or record the laws, stories, poems, and other literature, or the history and traditions of the people.

After Reading the Chapter

History

Have students work in cooperative-learning groups to brainstorm ideas for types of calendars other than the one we use. Then have them research other types of calendars people have used throughout history.

Art

Have students look at the picture of the clay tablet on page 37. Remind them that *cuneiform* means "wedge." If possible, provide students with some examples of cuneiform characters. Have students work in groups to make clay tablets. Then have them experiment with cuneiform writing.

Writing

Have students write one or two paragraphs comparing the laws of the Hebrews to the main idea of Hammurabi's laws—that the strong should not hurt the weak.

Foreign Languages

Have students research ancient alphabets and pictorial systems from around the world. Have students draw examples of letters and tell the class a little about the civilization that used the alphabet.

Chapter Summary Thousands of years ago, one of the world's greatest civilizations, ancient Egypt, developed along the Nile River. The Egyptians are well known for the building of the pyramids, as well as many other contributions to civilization.

Chapter Objectives Students will learn to

- identify the origins of the ancient Egyptian civilization.

- identify the organization of Egyptian government and society.

- identify Egyptian religious beliefs and practices, including mummification.

- identify examples of ancient Egypt's contributions to our society today.

Vocabulary

pharaoh, p. 44	pyramids, p. 46
mummification, p. 45	papyrus, p. 47
tomb, p. 45	hieroglyphics, p. 47

Vocabulary Activities List the following words on the chalkboard: *pharaoh, mummification, tomb, pyramid, papyrus, hieroglyphics.* Tell students that as they read this chapter, they will build a word web. You may use the Concept Web graphic organizer found on page 62 of this guide for this activity. Begin the web with the word *pharaoh.* Tell students that, as they read, they will add to this web. Remind students to use the glossary if they have difficulty with any of the vocabulary words.

Before Reading the Chapter Ask students what they know about ancient Egypt and, in particular, about pyramids and mummies. If any students have visited museums that have exhibits on the civilization of ancient Egypt, encourage them to describe what they saw. Display a book about King Tutankhamen. You may wish to show students pictures of furniture and other objects from Tutankhamen's tomb. Discuss with students how these objects are similar to furniture that we use today.

Teaching Suggestions and Answers

Page 43

Ask students to name some important rivers in the United States (the Mississippi, the Ohio, and the Rio Grande). Ask students if these rivers serve the same function for people as the Nile did for the ancient Egyptians. **Students should answer that the Sumerians and the Egyptians were able to farm near rivers. Plentiful food encouraged the growth of culture and civilization.**

Page 44

Students should answer that the Nile was important to Egypt because it was the only major river in Egypt that could provide water for growing crops. Mention that its importance was due to the fact that the rest of the land (except for the fertile strip along the Nile) was desert and not suitable for farming. Discuss with students the ways in which our society is different from that of ancient Egypt. (We elect our government officials and do not have a king or pharaoh.)

Page 45

Point out that mummies can provide scientists today with valuable information about the ancient Egyptians. Scientists can find out about the diseases the Egyptians suffered from and how long people lived in ancient times. They can even learn about the kinds of food the Egyptians ate. **Answers will vary. Some students might suggest that the Egyptians wanted to be remembered for things they had enjoyed doing in life. Others might suggest that since the Egyptians believed in an afterlife, they painted pictures of pleasant times and activities they expected to enjoy again in the afterlife.**

Page 46

Point out that there are more than 35 pyramids still standing in Egypt today. Explain that water from the Nile was often splashed under the stone blocks to make them slide more easily along the ramp. **Students should answer that they probably carried the stones by boat since the picture shows a dock and boats in the water near the pyramid.**

Page 47

Discuss with students what life would be like if calendars did not exist. (It would be difficult to keep track of time and plan for events.) Ask students to list various uses of paper. Remind students that in Mesopotamia writing was done on clay tablets. Discuss with them the advantages of using paper, rather than clay, to write on. **Answers should include that the fact that the mask was made of solid gold suggests that the pharaoh was rich, and therefore important.**

Page 48

Ask students how our written language is different from Egyptian hieroglyphics. (Our language uses letters that stand for sounds, while hieroglyphics use pictures that stand for sounds, ideas, objects, and actions.) **Students' answers may include hands, an owl, a vulture, and a sickle.**

Project Tip

Help students carry out the suggestion on page 48. You might bring in some books that contain pictures of Egyptian mummies or other artifacts of the Egyptians.

Page 49

Special People Discuss with students why people of one civilization would want to trade with people of other cultures or civilizations. **Answers might include intelligence, vision, compassion, and a sense of justice.**

Page 50

Chapter Checkup You may want to work through the Chapter Checkup with students.

Answers: 1. c **2.** a **3.** d **4.** a **5.** c **6.** b
Students might suggest that it is important to know about how other people lived and to learn what contributions they made.

After Reading the Chapter

Remind students of the importance of river valleys in Mesopotamia and Egypt. Students can use maps of your local area to assess the importance of rivers. They can then compare the geographic features of their own community with those of the two ancient civilizations.

Geography

Have students research and then write a report on the pyramids of Giza or the Sphinx. Encourage them to include information on the various theories on how they were built, and what the present Egyptian government is doing to protect them.

Language Arts

Ask students to find out more about hieroglyphics and to copy examples of their findings. Some students may enjoy making up a picture language of their own.

History

Have students research the life of another famous Egyptian pharaoh or queen, such as Ramses II, Akhenaton (Amenhotep IV—the religious revolutionary), Seti I, or Cleopatra VII. Have students arrange their findings on a biographical time line.

Writing

Tell students that as civilizations started in various parts of the world, people were anxious to exchange agricultural products and various objects of their culture with other peoples. Have students work in groups to write a story about a trading expedition from ancient Egypt to Sumer, Babylon, Syria, Lebanon, or Nubia. Have students determine which objects people would have had available to trade.

Architecture

Have students research and report about the Temples of Abu Simbel, shown in the photograph on page 43. Have students find out when and how the temples were built. Also have students report on why and how the temples were moved during the 1960s.

Recreation

People have played board games since ancient times. One of the oldest board games was found at Ur in Sumer. It is believed to be about 4,500 years old. Have students find out more about the board games used in Mesopotamia and in Egypt, such as the Egyptian game, "Hounds and Jackals." Students might enjoy designing their own board game, based on these ancient ones.

Chapter Summary The earliest civilizations in India and China developed in river valleys, as did the civilizations of Mesopotamia and Egypt. Civilization in India developed in the Indus River valley. Civilization in China developed in the Huang He (Yellow River) valley.

Chapter Objectives Students will learn to

- identify and describe India and China as centers of ancient civilizations.

- explain how archaeologists use artifacts to learn about the past.

- identify the Aryans and their effects on Indian civilization.

- describe the government and writing system of the ancient Chinese.

Vocabulary	
distance scale, p. 51	dynasty, p. 54
caste, p. 53	archaeology, p. 57
Hinduism, p. 53	

Vocabulary Activities Remind students that they probably already know the meanings of *biology* and *biologist*. These words are made up of two parts; both contain *bio-*, which means "life." Write the other two parts on the chalkboard: *-logy* means "the science or study of," and *-ist* means "one that specializes in a science." Tell students that they are now going to work out the meaning of *archaeology*. On the chalkboard, write that *archaeo-* means "ancient." Lead them to discover that *archaeology* means "the study of ancient or past cultures." Direct students who have difficulty with any of the terms to use the glossary.

Before Reading the Chapter Tell students that when we study ancient civilizations, we often cover a thousand years very quickly. They should try to keep in mind that a thousand years is really a long time. Ask students what they know about China today. Then point out that, like Sumer and Egypt, China also has an ancient civilization, dating back over five thousand years.

Teaching Suggestions and Answers

Page 51

Review why so many early civilizations began near rivers. (Rivers provide water for farming.) Have students look at the map on this page. Ask them how people might have traveled between the Fertile Crescent and the Indus River valley. (They probably traveled by boat, since the Tigris, Euphrates, and Indus rivers all empty into the ocean.) **Students should draw a line from where the Tigris River flows into the Indian Ocean to where the Indus River flows into the Indian Ocean. They should measure this distance. About 1,200 miles separate the Tigris River from the Indus River.**

Page 52

Tell students that archaeologists believe that Mohenjo-Daro was the capital city of a much larger state. Mohenjo-Daro itself covered about three miles of land. Explain that some of the most famous discoveries include works of art such as sculptures of bulls and buffalo and people dressed in elaborate headdresses. Discuss with students what can be learned by studying a civilization's artistic creations. **Students should answer that the high walls of Mohenjo-Daro provided protection against enemies.**

Page 53

Discuss with students why the Aryans considered fighters a higher caste than workers and farmers. What does that say about their culture? (The Aryans were a warlike people. They probably thought it was more important to be a good soldier than a farmer or worker.) **Students should answer that people in both Hindu and Egyptian cultures believed that people were born again after they died.**

Page 54

Discuss with students the difficulty of building a high wall in a mountainous region. Point out the similarities in the development of civilization in Egypt and China. For example, both civilizations began in a fertile valley and both used irrigation. **Students should answer that the part of the wall**

shown in the photo was built in a mountain region.

Page 55

Ask students how Chinese characters are similar to and different from cuneiform and hieroglyphic writing. (Chinese characters resemble objects, just as hieroglyphics do.) **Students should write the correct Chinese characters for the words** *tree* **and** *forest*.

Page 56

Point out that although Confucius was not widely known throughout China during his lifetime, his pupils spread his teachings after his death. His conversations and sayings were recorded in a book called the *Analects*. **Students' rules for helping people to lead a good life will vary.**

Project Tip

Help students carry out the suggestion on page 56. You might bring in some books that contain pictures of the lost city of Mohenjo-Daro. Students might make copies of pictures that interest them and then make models of cups, vases, and jewelry based on the pictures they have found.

Page 57

Around the Globe Explain that students who wish to become archaeologists must get a college degree. In college they will take courses in biology, history, languages, and geology. **Answers as to what might interest an archaeologist a thousand years from now will vary.**

Page 58

Chapter Checkup Work through the Chapter Checkup with students. Make sure all students understand what the correct answers are to the numbered questions.

Answers: 1. d **2.** c **3.** d **4.** a **5.** d **6.** d
Answers may vary. Civilizations were alike in that they began in river valleys. They were different in that they had different systems of writing and social organization.

After Reading the Chapter

Discuss with students the similarities and differences between the ancient civilizations of India and China.

Writing

Students can write about our civilization as if it were an ancient one. They can choose to research and write about areas such as technology, art, languages, religion, and law. They can put their material together in a book, along with illustrations cut from magazines.

Religion

Have students work in groups to make a comparison chart that lists the religious beliefs of the ancient civilizations they have studied. Their charts may include the name of the religion, the number of gods that were worshiped, laws or rules about life, ideas about life after death, and religious leaders, if any.

Writing

Have students read the teachings of Confucius. Have them combine his beliefs with their own beliefs to come up with five important rules about how people should live. Have them describe their rules in two or three paragraphs.

Architecture

Have students work in groups to find out more about the city of Mohenjo-Daro and its twin city of Harappa. Students might construct models or drawings of one of the cities.

Writing

Although the people of the Indus Valley did not leave behind any lengthy writings, they did develop and use a writing system. Archaeologists have found square stone seals with brief lines of writing and pictures of animals. Have students research to find pictures and more information about these seals. How and why were they used? Then have students use clay to design their own seals, using writing and pictures.

Chapter Summary Many scientists believe that humankind first began and developed in Africa. The ancient kingdoms of Kush, Axum, those of West Africa, and the empire of Mali are some of the important civilizations of Africa.

Chapter Objectives Students will learn to

- identify the early history of the inhabitants of the Sahara.

- differentiate among the ancient African kingdoms of Kush, Axum, Ghana, and Mali.

- locate important rivers, cities, and ancient kingdoms on a map of Africa.

Vocabulary

savannah, p. 60   sculpture, p. 65

caravan, p. 64

Vocabulary Activities Tell students that you are going to help them picture in their minds a *sculpture* of a *caravan* crossing a *savannah*. Tell them the sculpture, or statue, will be carved from wood. The grass growing on this African savannah is about knee-deep; there are few trees. The caravan is made up of many people riding camels. The leader rides an elephant. Then ask students to come up with definitions for *sculpture, caravan,* and *savannah*. Remind students who have any difficulty with the terms to use the glossary to find word meanings.

Before Reading the Chapter Ask students to review what they learned in Chapter 2 about deserts. Discuss with the class what it would be like to live in a desert. What human needs would be difficult to meet? Tell students that art is an important element of civilization. Inform them that a work of art may be a practical item, such as a building or a hand tool, as well as a statue or a painting. Have them discuss what art means to them in terms of public buildings, homes, paintings, carvings, and so forth. They may want to discuss art in their everyday lives, beginning with the design of your school. Have students look at the map on page 60. Briefly discuss the names

on the map to familiarize students with the places they will be studying.

Teaching Suggestions and Answers
Page 59
Students' answers about other civilizations that have built walls around their cities should include Mesopotamia and China.

Page 60
Ask students the name of the only river that runs through the desert region of the Sahara. (the Nile) **Students should trace the borders of both the Sahara and the savannah.** After students have traced the borders of the Sahara and the savannah, you might have them trace the borders of the rain forest.

Page 61
Discuss with students why the Kingdom of Kush might have begun where it did, on the banks of the Nile. (The people of Kush needed water from the Nile for their crops, just as the Egyptians did.) **Students should answer that the Kush pyramids differed from those in Egypt because they have flat rather than pointed tops.**

Page 62
Have students look at the map on page 60. Then ask them to name the two bodies of water that helped make Axum a good trading city. (the Nile River and the Red Sea) **Answers should include that the people of Axum, like the people of Kush, traded goods and tamed elephants.**

Page 63
Discuss with students why the leaders of Ghana kept the location of their gold a secret. (If the traders who came to Ghana had known the location of the gold, they might have tried taking the gold by force instead of trading salt for it.) **Students should answer that gold has high value and can be traded for other goods.**

Project Tip
Help students carry out the suggestion on page 63. If possible, you might locate similar

illustrations showing trade caravans in books about Africa and display them to the class. You might suggest that the students include their own drawings in the museum display for the unit project.

Page 64

Have students look at the map on page 60. Then ask: Near what river is Timbuktu located? (the Niger River) Have students use the distance scale on the map to estimate the distance between Timbuktu and Cairo. (about 2,200 miles) **Students should circle Timbuktu.**

Page 65

For Your Information Ask students if they think that African artists might have made sculptures out of gold. (Gold was in plentiful supply in the kingdoms of Ghana and Mali. African artists probably used gold to make sculpture and other works of art.) **Students might mention the long face and neck, the long nose, and the eyes of similar shape.**

Page 66

Chapter Checkup You may want to work through the Chapter Checkup with students. Make sure they all understand what the correct answers are to the numbered questions.

Answers: 1. c **2.** b **3.** b **4.** d **5.** d **6.** b
Answers will vary.

After Reading the Chapter

Discuss with students the different civilizations of ancient Africa. Encourage volunteers to describe to the class the characteristics of each of these civilizations.

Art
Using the description on page 62, have students draw a picture of the King of Axum as they think he would look and would dress. Encourage students to show the wealth and beauty of the king's court in Axum.

Geography
Have the class study a current map of Africa. Which countries are now located in the regions studied in this chapter? Have students make a chart to show what countries can be found today in the regions where Kush, Axum, Ghana, and Mali once flourished.

Writing
Have students do some research to find out more about camels. Then have them write a story set in one of the ancient African kingdoms in which a camel is the main character. They might choose to give their camel human characteristics or they might prefer to describe it more realistically.

History
Have students work in teams to create a book about one of the ancient civilizations they have studied. The team could decide on the design and layout of the book. Then they could divide the task of gathering information. Some team members could copy pictures from magazines, encyclopedias, and art books that show what the people, clothes, art, and buildings of the time were like. The other team members would write the narrative for each of the picture displays.

Writing
Have students imagine that they are travelers in Africa. Have them plan a journey to one of the African kingdoms mentioned in the chapter. Ask students to imagine that they spend three days visiting one of these kingdoms. Have them write a journal entry for each day of their visit. They should describe the kind of transportation they use, the land they travel through, the cities where they stay, and the people and cultures they meet.

Unit Summary The civilizations of classical Greece and Rome provided a recognizable foundation for our own democratic society. After the fall of Rome, feudalism brought order to Europe. During the Renaissance and Reformation, more people began to move from feudal manors to cities. New ideas spread throughout Europe as a result of inventions such as the printing press. As the feudal system weakened, modern European nations began to emerge. In the 1700s, the Industrial Revolution changed life in Europe forever.

Before Reading the Unit Introduce the unit by showing students the following areas on a map or globe: Greece, Rome, and Europe.

Have students study the unit opener on page 69. Ask them what they remember about the kinds of governments that existed in ancient Egypt and China. Encourage students to think about the questions as they read the unit.

Point out the Unit Project box to students and explain that they will work on this project as they read through the unit.

Unit Project

Setting Up the Project Divide the class into pairs of news reporters. Suggest to partners that for each historical event they choose to report on they should work to get answers to each of the following questions: Who? What? Where? When? Why? How? They can use the information they gather by asking these questions to prepare their live broadcast.

Students will find specific suggestions in the Project Tip sections of the chapters. Encourage them to adapt the suggestions to their own interests.

Presenting the Project One alternative possibility might be for students to make a collage showing the scenes and figures from history they have discussed in their reports. The collage could be illustrated with copies of pictures from books, magazines, and encyclopedias.

After Reading the Unit Invite discussion of the questions on the unit opener and the answers students discovered about the rise of the West. Prompt discussion by asking questions such as: What form of government evolved in the West?

What contributions did Greece and Rome make to later European civilization?

Skill Builder
Using a Time Line
As students read page 102, remind them that a time line is useful for finding out quickly the order of past events.

Answers: 1. fall of Roman Empire **2.** 800 **3.** Students should mark 1187 on the time line and add the label *Muslims recapture Jerusalem* **4.** 717 **5.** Students should bracket the time span from 476 to 1500 in some way and indicate with a label that those years are the Middle Ages.

Bibliography

Teacher
Europe at the Time of Greece and Rome. (History of the World Series) Steck-Vaughn, 1988. (Grades 5–6)

Garland, Robert. *The Greek Way of Life: From Conception to Old Age.* Cornell Univ. Press, 1990.

Harris, Nataniel. *Renaissance Art.* (Art and Artists Series) Thomson Learning, 1994. (Grades 6–7)

Knight, Khadijan. *Islam.* (World Religions Series) Thomson Learning, 1995. (Grades 4–8)

Student
Coote, Roger. *The Anglo-Saxons.* (Look Into the Past Series) Thomson Learning, 1995. (Grades 4–6)

Hull, Robert. *Greek Stories.* (Tales From Around the World) Thomson Learning, 1994. (Grades 5–6)

Hull, Robert. *Roman Stories.* (Tales From Around the World) Thomson Learning, 1994. (Grades 5–6)

Williams, A. Susan. *The Greeks.* (Look Into the Past Series) Thomson Learning, 1993. (Grades 4–6)

Teacher's Resource Binder

Blackline Masters for Unit 3: Unit 3 Project Organizer, Unit 3 Review, Unit 3 Test; Activities for Chapters 8, 9, 10, 11; Outline Maps of the World, Europe

Chapter Summary Greek civilization was very different from the civilizations of Egypt and Mesopotamia. Life in ancient Greece centered around the Aegean Sea. The Greeks established colonies and built city-states throughout the Aegean. Their democratic form of government was the model for our own government.

Chapter Objectives Students will learn to

- identify ways in which sailing and trading contributed to the development of the Greek civilization.

- identify city-states and compare Sparta with Athens.

- describe the origins of democracy, theater, and the Olympic games in Greece.

- locate Greek colonies and Mount Olympus on a map.

Vocabulary	
colonies, p. 71	democracy, p. 73
citizens, p. 73	tragedies, p. 75
agora, p. 73	comedies, p. 75

Vocabulary Activities Write the word *city-state* on the chalkboard, and ask students to suggest what it might mean. Tell them that ancient Greece was divided into city-states, each with its own government. Ask students to imagine what our nation would be like if each city or each state had its own army, its own laws, even its own money. On a world map, compare the size of Greece to that of the United States. Would this make it harder or easier to have separate governments? Remind students who are having trouble with any of the terms to use the glossary.

Before Reading the Chapter Explain to students that life in ancient Greece was centered around the Aegean Sea. Since Greece lacked farmland, the ancient Greeks depended on the sea for food. Greece also lacked certain natural resources such as mineral deposits. The Greeks became expert sailors and depended on overseas trade for the goods they needed. Ask if anyone

in the class has ever seen fishing boats being unloaded on a dock. If so, ask them to describe the scene to the class. If not, ask the class to imagine the sights, sounds, and smells of a harbor.

Teaching Suggestions and Answers
Page 70

Point out that there are more than 2,000 islands in the Aegean Sea. Most of these are inhabited. One reason that Greece was able to create a rich civilization was that it was located at the crossroads of many different cultures. The Greeks could learn from all the different peoples with whom they came in contact. Make sure students understand that classical Greece is the same as ancient Greece. **Students should name the Mediterranean, Ionian, and Aegean seas.**

Page 71

Ask students to look at the map on this page and name a mountain in Greece. (Mt. Olympus) Point out to students that the remains of ancient ships have been found at the bottom of the sea near Greece. Scientists have studied them and built a modern model of the ancient ships. **Students should circle the areas that were controlled by Greece.**

Page 72

Discuss with students why governing a city might be easier than governing a large nation. (A city is much smaller than a nation. It might be easier to organize and construct new buildings and other projects.) **Answers should include the idea that the Spartans had confidence in their ability to defend their city.**

Project Tip
Help students carry out the suggestion on page 72. If possible, you might locate books about ancient Sparta that the students can use to find examples of art and information to accompany their news stories.

Page 73

Discuss with students whether modern cities have areas that are similar to the agora in ancient Athens. (Most cities and towns have some kind of central market or shopping area.) Discuss the differences between Athenian democracy and that of the present-day United States. Be sure that students understand that only men who had been born in Athens could vote. Ask students to name those who could not vote (women, men who had been born in other cities). **Answers might mention oranges and grapes as two kinds of fruit they might find in the agora. In comparing how Athens and Sparta raised their sons, students should mention that in Sparta the boys were raised in camps, and taught to use weapons and to follow orders. In Athens the children were trained to be good students, athletes, and citizens as well as soldiers.**

Page 74

Discuss with students why a goddess of wisdom would have been important to the Athenians. (The Athenians were interested in government and ideas; wisdom would have been important to them.) Point out that Socrates never wrote down any of his teachings. He believed that people should be taught directly through conversation. It was left to his students to write down his teachings. Almost all that we know of Socrates comes from the writings of his student Plato. **Students should answer that Socrates asked questions but he did not give the answers. He wanted people to think for themselves.**

Page 75

Point out that the Olympic games were first celebrated in 776 B.C. in the city of Olympia, Greece. The games originally lasted one day and consisted only of a footrace. Later, other contests were added, such as the javelin throw, the long jump, boxing and wrestling matches, and chariot races. Winners at the games became national heroes. The modern Olympics began in 1896. A French baron, Pierre de Coubertin, was largely responsible for their revival. Coubertin believed that international competition among amateur athletes would decrease world tensions. The winter games were added in 1924. **Students should answer that the Olympic games were held every four years in ancient Greece.**

Page 76

Around the Globe Point out that, like the Greeks, the Phoenicians learned to make swift sailing ships. These ships were powered by large sails and teams of rowers. The Phoenicians were excellent sailors. They even built lighthouses to mark the way on their voyages. Like Greece, Phoenicia had poor farmland, so the people became traders and obtained food through trade with other countries. Discuss with students how trading during ancient times helped people find out about new ideas. (They learned about new ideas and products by trading with other civilizations.) **Answers should include ivory tusks.**

Page 77

Chapter Checkup You may want to work through the Chapter Checkup with students.

Answers: 1. b **2.** a **3.** b **4.** d **5.** a **6.** c
Answers will vary, but students should mention that Sparta was controlled by the army and conquered other lands. Athens was a democracy and became rich by trading with other lands.

After Reading the Chapter

Art
Have students make a bulletin-board display entitled "The Glory of Greece." Explain that Greece left the world many beautiful works of art. Have students look for pictures of Greek buildings and works of art in magazines and travel brochures.

Geography
Have students work in cooperative-learning groups to plan a trip to visit the sites of ancient Greece. Students could write to a travel agent requesting information about Greece. They might also use pictures from magazines or drawings to make a travel brochure describing the sites they will visit.

Reading
Have groups of students read an illustrated Greek myth together. Then have each group make a poster of a scene from the myth. Display the posters in the classroom or have groups retell the myth for another group, using their poster as a visual aid.

Making a Time Line
Have students work in small groups to research important dates in Greek history. Then have students create an illustrated time line using pictures or drawings. Their time lines should begin with 776 B.C. and end with 146 B.C. when Greece was conquered by the Romans.

Chapter Summary The ideas of Greece helped shape Roman civilization. Rome began as a republic but eventually became an empire ruled by emperors. The birth of Jesus Christ occurred during the reign of the emperor Augustus Caesar. For a long time, Christianity was against the law in the Roman Empire. The emperor Constantine made Christianity legal.

Chapter Objectives Students will learn to

- compare Rome to Greece, in terms of geographic advantages.

- identify Roman rule over its citizens, and the Roman Empire.

- identify connections between the Roman Empire and Christianity.

- distinguish between A.D. and B.C. dates.

Vocabulary

empire, p. 78	emperor, p. 82
republic, p. 80	Pax Romana, p. 82
patricians, p. 80	Christianity, p. 82
plebeians, p. 80	legal, p. 82
dictators, p. 81	aqueducts, p. 84

Vocabulary Activities Write the following pairs of words on the chalkboard: *empire* and *republic; patricians* and *plebeians; dictator* and *emperor.* Have students find the meanings for each pair of words and then tell the rest of the class how the pairs are alike and how they are different. Help students who have difficulty with the terms use the glossary.

Before Reading the Chapter Point out the map on page 79. Have students compare it with the map of Greece on page 71. Ask students to explain what seems to have happened in the region between the years 450 B.C. and A.D. 200. Tell them that in this chapter they will read about the development of the Roman Empire. Remind students that throughout history many nations and leaders have fought wars to gain control over other areas.

Teaching Suggestions and Answers

Page 78

Students should answer that Athens is about 650 miles from Rome.

Page 79

Tell students that the story of Romulus and Remus is part of the mythology of Rome. Like many people, the Romans told stories and myths to explain things that could not be explained otherwise. **Students should answer that, from Rome, London was northwest, Carthage was southwest, the Danube was northeast, and Egypt was southeast.**

Page 80

Discuss with students ways in which the early Roman Republic was similar to our form of government in the United States. (In both, the people chose their own leaders.)

Students may need help pronouncing the words *patricians* and *plebeians.* Ask students why trade was so important to people who lived near the Mediterranean. (Trade supplied people with products they might not have had in their own countries.) **Students should answer that Carthage is about 400 miles from Rome.**

Page 81

Tell students that after Julius Caesar's death, his grandnephew Augustus searched for the men who had killed Caesar. This was one reason he earned the title "respected one." **Students should answer that the Romans were afraid of being ruled by a king again because they had been ruled by many corrupt kings.**

Project Tip

Help students carry out the suggestion on page 81. You might read to the class a more detailed description of Hannibal's journey over the Alps and descent into Italy from a history book or an encyclopedia article.

Page 82

Discuss with students why it would have been important to the Romans to have people who lived in the empire serve in the Roman Army.

(Many people were needed to protect the borders of the empire.) Point out to students that the personal name of Jesus Christ was Jesus. The term *Christ* is a title closely associated with Jesus, so it became part of his name. It comes from the Greek word *Christos,* which means "anointed one" or "special." Point out that no one really knows what Jesus or Mary looked like, and that these pictures are artists' interpretations. **Students should answer that followers of Judaism and Christianity believed in only one God, while the religions of ancient civilizations had many gods.**

Page 83

Review the B.C. and A.D. systems of dating by asking students which of these events happened first, an event in 450 B.C. or an event in 750 B.C. (750 B.C.). Then ask students which of these events happened first, an event in A.D. 1100 or one in A.D. 1200 (A.D. 1100). **Students should answer that the first Olympic games were held 776 years before Jesus was born; 464 years passed between the date when the first Olympic games were held and the date when work on the first Roman road began; three centuries passed between the birth of Jesus and the end of the persecution of the Christians; 1,000 years passed between the formation of the Greek city-states and the beginning of the persecution of the Christians.**

Page 84

For Your Information Students should answer that the English word is *second.*

Page 85

Chapter Checkup Work through the Chapter Checkup with students. Make sure all students understand what the correct answers are to the numbered questions.

Answers: 1. d **2.** b **3.** d **4.** c **5.** a **6.** c Answers will vary, but might include that the Caesars were not quite as strong as the other rulers. They made some attempts to keep their people contented. For example, Julius Caesar promised to find jobs for poor people. Augustus Caesar made sure that Rome and its empire were ruled fairly. The other rulers didn't have to answer to their people.

After Reading the Chapter

Geography
Have students find out more about Roman roads. Why were roads so important to the Romans? Make copies of a map of the Roman Empire and distribute to students. Have them use an encyclopedia or books about Rome to find out how Roman roads were made. Then have students draw important roads on the map.

Writing
Have students write a diary entry. Tell them to imagine that they are with Hannibal's army as it crosses the Alps. Students should try to imagine and record what a soldier in Hannibal's army might have seen or experienced in the course of a day.

Drama
Students can apply what they have learned about tragedy or comedy and work in groups to write a play. Settings could include Hannibal's entry into Rome or the death of Julius Caesar. Students can read their plays aloud or stage particular scenes.

Making a Time Line
Have students make an illustrated time line of the history of Rome from its founding date, to the fall of the Roman Empire in A.D. 476.

Architecture
Have students work in groups to research and make a drawing or a model of any of the following: the home of a patrician, the Roman Forum, a Roman warship, the Appian Way, an arch, a vault, or the Colosseum. Students should include a short written or oral report with their models or drawings.

Religion
Have students find out about Roman gods and goddesses. Have them make a chart or table listing the name of the god or goddess, the aspect of life with which they were associated, and the Greek counterpart of each god or goddess. Students may then wish to tell the class a myth about one of the gods or goddesses.

Chapter Summary The Roman Empire came to an end in A.D. 476. The years between 476 and 1500 are known as the Middle Ages. A system of government called feudalism arose during the Middle Ages. The Crusades that occurred between 1096–1291 changed Europe in many important ways and influenced the growth of towns and trade between Europe and the East.

Chapter Objectives Students will learn to

- describe the rise of feudalism.
- identify the importance of Christianity and the role of the Roman Catholic Church during the Middle Ages.
- locate on a map various routes of the Crusades.
- identify the influence of the Crusades on the growth of towns and trade in Europe.

Vocabulary

feudalism, p. 87	nuns, p. 89
nobles, p. 87	cathedrals, p. 89
vassals, p. 87	Muslims, p. 90
knights, p. 87	pope, p. 90
serfs, p. 87	Crusades, p. 90
manor, p. 88	guilds, p. 91
monks, p. 89	

Vocabulary Activities Have students use the vocabulary words to write a summary of the Middle Ages. You might want to help students get started by giving them the following sentence: "In the system of *feudalism, nobles* were rich men of the upper class." Remind students who have difficulty with any of the terms to use the glossary.

Before Reading the Chapter Have students locate the continent of Europe on a globe or map. Call on students to describe its location in relation to the other six continents. Then have them look at the map of the Roman Empire on page 79. Have them identify which present-day European countries were formed from lands controlled by Rome over 1,500 years ago. Tell them that in this chapter, they will read about what happened in Europe after the government in Rome collapsed. Ask students to explain what happened to the teachings of Jesus after his death. Remind them that in A.D. 313, Christianity became the official religion of the Roman Empire. Explain that in this chapter, they will read about the role of the church after the fall of Rome.

Teaching Suggestions and Answers
Page 86
Answers should include language, law, and the building of roads and aqueducts.

Page 87
Explain to students that, from childhood, many of the male children of nobles were trained to become knights. They began their training as pages at the age of 7. Pages grew up in the noble's castle, where they served as messengers. When a page was 14 years old, he became a squire. Squires took care of a knight's horse and polished his armor. The squire was also taught how to ride a horse and how to use a sword. If a squire did well, he was made a knight when he was about 20 years old. **Students should answer that both were vassals and had knights.**

Page 88
Point out that feudalism became the common way of life in the Middle Ages because there was a constant threat of attack. A noble's manor always had to be prepared for war. Ask students what the presence of a church on a feudal manor suggests about the spread of Christianity after the fall of the Roman Empire. (Christianity continued to spread even after the fall of Rome.) **Answers will vary.**

Page 89
Tell students that cathedrals were often called "Bibles for the poor." Since many people who lived during the Middle Ages were unable to read, the stained-glass windows were lessons in Christian history. Mention that cathedrals took

many years to build. The Cathedral of Notre Dame in Paris was built over a period of 87 years. **Students should answer that he is copying a book by hand.**

Project Tip
Help students carry out the suggestion on page 89. Students can supplement their reports with scenes of manors that they might have seen in movies that were set in medieval times. Scenes they recall from such movies will add color and detail to their reports.

Page 90
Point out to students that the Latin name for cross, *crux*, gave these journeys their name—the *Crusades*. Explain that there were several Crusades from 1096 to 1291. When they ended, Europe did not have any control in the Middle East. **Answers should include that religion was very important during the Middle Ages. Also, since Jesus lived in Jerusalem, it was considered a holy city.**

Page 91
Have students look at the map on this page. Ask them to name two cities the Crusaders passed through on their way to Jerusalem. (Constantinople, Antioch, Acre, Rome) Point out to students that during the Children's Crusade in 1212, children from Germany and France became convinced that God would deliver Jerusalem to them because they were poor and weak. Thousands of children began the journey to Jerusalem, but most of them died from starvation on the way. Others were captured and sold into slavery by the Muslims. **Students should trace the route of the first Crusade.**

Page 92
Special People Tell students that Charlemagne was the last great ruler in Europe after the fall of Rome. After his death his empire fell apart. This resulted in conditions that eventually led to the development of feudalism, which students learned about earlier in the chapter. **Answers should include that Charlemagne started schools and governed fairly.**

Page 93
Chapter Checkup You may want to work through the Chapter Checkup with students.

Answers: 1. a **2.** c **3.** a **4.** b **5.** d **6.** a
Answers will vary, but should include that priests learned Latin, the language of the church; they taught others Latin; nuns and monks copied the books of ancient Greece and Rome and helped to keep learning alive at this time.

After Reading the Chapter
Geography
Have students work in groups to find on a map or globe the area covered by ancient Palestine. Have them calculate the distance from England to Jerusalem, and from France to Jerusalem.

Art
Have students make "stained-glass windows." Students can create designs with outlines on black construction paper, and then can cut out the outlines. The areas that have been cut out can then be filled with colored-cellophane "stained glass." Students can demonstrate the "Bible-for-the-poor" idea of cathedral stained-glass windows by having theirs teach a lesson.

History
Have students work in groups to study and make a bulletin-board display about one of the following topics: armor in the Middle Ages; the Children's Crusade; the great cathedrals of Europe, music or entertainment (the troubadours, tournaments).

Writing
Have students research and write a brief biography of two or three paragraphs about one of the following leaders of the Crusades: Saladin (the Muslim leader), Richard the Lion-Hearted, Godfrey of Bouillon, Raymond of Toulouse, or Robert of Flanders.

Chapter Summary By the 1300s, some Europeans began to look again at the ideas of the Greeks and Romans. This rediscovery of past ideas was the beginning of the Renaissance. Many exceptional artists and thinkers flourished during this time. The feudal system weakened, and during the 1500s and 1600s, people began to think of themselves as members of nations rather than as citizens of towns. In the 1700s, new inventions made it possible to mass-produce goods. New industries sprang up and the Industrial Revolution began.

Chapter Objectives Students will learn to

- identify the hallmarks of the Renaissance and name two important artists of the period.

- identify the Reformation and explain why its ideas were able to spread quickly.

- locate the new nations of Europe on a map.

- identify the causes and effects of the Industrial Revolution.

Vocabulary

Protestants, p. 96	textiles, p. 98
nation, p. 97	Industrial Revolution, p. 99
common law, p. 98	
Magna Carta, p. 98	armada, p. 100

Vocabulary Activities On the chalkboard list all the vocabulary terms. Then make a time line spanning the years 1000 to 1800. As students read the chapter, help them assign years or time periods that relate to the terms. For instance, place the term *Magna Carta* at 1215. When you study Martin Luther, remind students that Protestantism began with Luther. Students may choose to place the term *Protestants* at 1520, the year Luther left the Roman Catholic Church. Remind students to use the glossary to find meanings for any words they find difficult.

Before Reading the Chapter Ask students if they have ever visited a museum and seen sculptures from ancient Greece and Rome. Ask students to describe the statues. Explain that in this chapter, they will read how these statues influenced European artists at the end of the Middle Ages.

Teaching Suggestions and Answers

Page 94

Have students look at the picture on this page. Point out the wall that surrounds the city of Florence. Review with students that many cities founded before or during the Middle Ages had walls around them for protection. **Students should mention Athens in ancient Greece.**

Page 95

Review the achievements of ancient Greece and Rome with students. Discuss why their achievements might have been valued by thinkers like Petrarch. **Students should answer that people developed new ideas by studying the past.**

Page 96

Point out to students that Johannes Gutenberg invented the printing press in the mid-1400s in Germany. This was one reason Luther's ideas spread so quickly. Gutenberg's printing press used small pieces of metal, or movable type. Each piece had a single letter of the alphabet. The metal pieces could be placed in trays to form lines of print. In this way, Gutenberg could print 300 pages a day. **Students should answer that the printing press was an important invention because it enabled ideas to be spread more quickly.**

Project Tip
Help students carry out the suggestion on page 96. You might bring to class visual depictions of Luther's famous action and show them to students. This might enable them to write a more vivid news report.

Page 97

Students should answer that Rome was a city in the Papal States.

Page 98

Ask students to name the head of the government in the United States. (the President) Does the President have to obey the same laws as everyone else? (yes) **Students should answer that both apply to everyone.**

Page 99

Use the Cause and Effect graphic organizer found on page 64 of this guide to record the causes of the Industrial Revolution and the effects it had on individuals and society. Discuss the plight of workers and children during the Industrial Revolution. Explain that during the 18th century, children also worked on farms, but on farms children usually worked with their parents. In cities, children usually worked in one place while their parents worked in another. They worked long hours, often for extremely low wages. Many of the factories were dangerous. Both children and adults were sometimes injured or killed by unsafe equipment. In the 1860s, many child labor laws went into effect in England that made employing young children in factories against the law. **Students should answer that a revolution describes a major and important change. The Industrial Revolution changed forever the way the people worked.**

Page 100

Special People Discuss why Queen Elizabeth had the support of her people. (She was a good leader; under her rule England became one of the most powerful nations in the world; she encouraged artists and writers; she traveled through the land to see the people.) Explain that in 1574 Elizabeth freed all the serfs in England. This meant they did not have to stay on a manor if they did not want to. It was another change that marked modern times—the idea that everyone has a right to freedom. **Students should answer that the Spanish gave up because the English Navy set fire to their own ships and then began to attack the Spanish Armada.**

Page 101

Chapter Checkup You may want to work through the Chapter Checkup with students.

Answers: 1. d **2.** c **3.** a **4.** c **5.** a **6.** b
Answers will vary, but should include that new factories attracted workers. People left their farms to take jobs in the new factories, which were located in towns and cities which then continued to grow.

After Reading the Chapter

Writing

To emphasize the importance of the Magna Carta, have students draw up a bill of rights. Discuss why it is important to establish people's rights and to limit the power of the ruler. Then divide the class into groups of three or four. Have each group write up its own bill of rights, which it will then present to the rest of the class.

Science

Tell students that Leonardo da Vinci designed machines and drew plans for hundreds of inventions, many of which were centuries ahead of their time. Have groups of interested students find out more about some of Leonardo da Vinci's inventions. Students may draw diagrams of some of the inventions or explain to the class how one of Leonardo's inventions was designed to work.

Mid-Term Test

The mid-term test on the following three pages covers Units 1–3, Chapters 1–11.

Answers: 1. c **2.** a **3.** b **4.** d **5.** c **6.** a **7.** b **8.** c **9.** d **10.** b **11.** a **12.** d **13.** d **14.** b **15.** a **16.** c **17.** d **18.** c **19.** b **20.** a **21.** b **22.** d **23.** c **24.** b **25.** d **26.** a **27.** b **28.** c **29.** d **30.** c

Mid-Term Test

Finish each sentence. Circle the letter in front of the correct answer.

1. All the natural things (such as deserts, seas, and rivers) that exist in a place are part of the
   a. community.
   b. economy.
   c. natural environment.
   d. culture.

2. The way a people choose their leaders and make their laws is their
   a. government.
   b. economy.
   c. culture.
   d. environment.

3. The tools, materials, and knowledge people use to make things is called
   a. transportation.
   b. technology.
   c. community.
   d. economy.

4. How hot, cold, wet, or dry a place is year after year is called its
   a. region.
   b. plateau.
   c. erosion.
   d. climate.

5. Huge sheets of ice are called
   a. deserts.
   b. plateaus.
   c. glaciers.
   d. plains.

6. Moisture that falls on the earth is called
   a. precipitation.
   b. erosion.
   c. lava.
   d. climate.

7. Oil and coal are examples of
   a. tools.
   b. fuels.
   c. pollution.
   d. machines.

8. Trees provide us with the important resource of
   a. electricity.
   b. food.
   c. lumber.
   d. gas.

9. A chemical used to kill mosquitoes that also killed birds and insects was
   a. oil.
   b. gas.
   c. petroleum.
   d. DDT.

10. The dirtying of Earth's air and water is called
    a. energy.
    b. pollution.
    c. conservation.
    d. renewable resources.

Mid-Term Test (continued)

11. Land that is good for farming is

    a. fertile.
    b. domesticated.
    c. mountainous.
    d. conserved.

12. Cuneiform was a system of writing invented by

    a. the Egyptians.
    b. the Caesars.
    c. Petrarch.
    d. the Sumerians.

13. The Mesopotamian leader who developed a set of laws was

    a. Abraham.
    b. Moses.
    c. Sumer.
    d. Hammurabi.

14. The ruler of Egypt was called the

    a. emperor.
    b. pharaoh.
    c. king.
    d. governor.

15. Embalmed bodies placed in tombs in ancient Egypt were called

    a. mummies.
    b. pharaohs.
    c. pyramids.
    d. hieroglyphics.

16. The first woman to become pharaoh was

    a. Menes.
    b. Ra.
    c. Hatshepsut.
    d. Tutankhamen.

17. An ancient ruined city discovered in the Indus River valley was called

    a. Aryan.
    b. Huang He.
    c. Hinduism.
    d. Mohenjo-Daro.

18. One of China's greatest teachers, who lived 2,500 years ago, was

    a. Huang He.
    b. Aryan.
    c. Confucius.
    d. Mohenjo-Daro.

19. The grasslands of Africa are called the

    a. Sahara.
    b. savannah.
    c. rain forest.
    d. caravan.

20. Meroe was the capital city of the African kingdom of

    a. Kush.
    b. Axum.
    c. Ghana.
    d. Mali.

Mid-Term Test (continued)

21. The Greek city-state that had the best army in Greece and trained its children to defend it was

    a. Athens.
    b. Sparta.
    c. Phoenicia.
    d. Acropolis.

22. One of the wisest men in Athens, who was sentenced to death, was

    a. Plato.
    b. Athena.
    c. Parthenon.
    d. Socrates.

23. A large area of land with many different people controlled by one person or a small group is called

    a. a city-state.
    b. a republic.
    c. an empire.
    d. a civilization.

24. The first emperor of Rome was

    a. Julius Caesar.
    b. Augustus Caesar.
    c. Hannibal.
    d. Romulus.

25. A general from Carthage who attacked the Romans was

    a. Remus.
    b. Julius Caesar.
    c. Augustus Caesar.
    d. Hannibal.

26. In the Middle Ages, someone who farmed the land was a

    a. serf.
    b. noble.
    c. vassal.
    d. knight.

27. Large, beautiful churches built during the Middle Ages were called

    a. temples.
    b. cathedrals.
    c. manors.
    d. guilds.

28. Charlemagne's empire was called

    a. the Roman Empire.
    b. the Crusades.
    c. the Holy Roman Empire.
    d. feudalism.

29. In 1215, English nobles forced King John to sign a paper limiting the king's power, called the

    a. common law.
    b. Reformation.
    c. Industrial Revolution.
    d. Magna Carta.

30. The English Navy under Queen Elizabeth defeated the

    a. Reformation.
    b. Magna Carta.
    c. Spanish Armada.
    d. Industrial Revolution.

Unit Summary The Eastern Hemisphere stretches from Europe and Africa across to Japan and to the southern Pacific Islands. The five continents of the Eastern Hemisphere contain the world's largest desert and tallest mountain. The nations of Europe have had a lasting effect on the cultures of many nations in the Eastern Hemisphere.

Before Reading the Unit Introduce the unit by asking students if they can identify the continents of Africa, Europe, Asia, and Australia on a globe or a map. (You may wish to point out the map of the Eastern Hemisphere on page 105.) Which nations can students name on these continents? Which ancient civilizations have they read about that began on these continents?

Have students open their books to the unit opener on page 104. Encourage students to think about the questions as they read the unit.

Draw students' attention to the Unit Project box and explain that they will work on this project as they read through the unit.

Unit Project

Setting Up the Project Divide the class into groups of travel guides. For each country in the Eastern Hemisphere that students plan to visit on their tour, they can record information about the following topics: political leaders; culture (music, dance, theater, art); architecture; food; geography. They can use this information to plan their tour.

Students will find specific suggestions in the Project Tip sections of the chapters. Encourage students to adapt the suggestions to their own interests.

Presenting the Project One alternative possibility might be to make a table display or a bulletin-board display of all the brochures created by the teams. In this way, individual students can browse through the brochures as time allows.

After Reading the Unit Invite discussion of the questions on the unit opener and the answers students discovered about the Eastern Hemisphere. Prompt discussion by asking questions such as: What continents make up the Eastern Hemisphere? What ancient civilizations and cultures arose in the Eastern Hemisphere?

Skill Builder

Reading a Double Line Graph

As students read page 162, remind them that when two lines are on the same graph, you can make comparisons between the lines.

Answers: 1. no **2.** 600 million **3.** 1985 **4.** Students will probably say yes. The graph shows that India had a population of about 900 million in 1995. India grew by about 200 million between 1985 and 1995. If it grows at the same rate, it will top one billion by 2010 or earlier.

Bibliography

Teacher

Darien-Smith, Kate, and David Lowe. *The Australian Outback and Its People.* (People and Places Series) Thomson Learning, 1995. (Grades 5–6)

Hull, Robert. *Indian Stories.* (Tales From Around the World Series) Thomson Learning, 1994. (Grades 5–6)

MacDonald, Robert. *Maori.* (Threatened Cultures Series) Thomson Learning, 1994. (Grades 5–6)

Student

Doran, Clare. *The Japanese.* (Look Into the Past Series) Thomson Learning, 1994. (Grades 4–6)

Gutnik, Martin J. and Natalie Browne-Gutnik. *Great Barrier Reef.* (Wonders of the World Series) Raintree Steck-Vaughn, 1995. (Grades 6–7)

Nile, Richard. *Australian Aborigines.* (Threatened Cultures Series) Raintree/Steck-Vaughn, 1993. (Grades 5–6)

Pischel, Enrica Collotti. *China from the 7th to the 19th Century.* (History of the World Series) Steck-Vaughn, 1994. (Grades 5–6)

Scoones, Simon. *The Sahara and Its People.* (People and Places Series) Thomson Learning, 1995. (Grades 5–6)

Teacher's Resource Binder

Blackline Masters for Unit 4: Unit 4 Project Organizer, Unit 4 Review, Unit 4 Test; Activities for Chapters 12, 13, 14, 15, 16, 17; Outline Maps of the World, Hemispheres

Chapter Summary The Eastern Hemisphere is made up of the continents of Europe, Russia, Asia, and Africa. Climate and geography affect the way people live in the different parts of the Eastern Hemisphere.

Chapter Objectives Students will learn to

- use parallels and meridians to locate places on maps.

- distinguish among the climates and geographic features of Europe, Russia, South Asia, and North Africa.

- identify the effect of the Gulf Stream on Europe, and the effect of monsoons on South Asia.

Vocabulary

hemispheres, p. 105	peninsula, p. 107
Prime Meridian, p. 105	current, p. 107
	tundra, p. 108
lines of latitude, p. 106	monsoons, p. 109
lines of longitude, p. 106	oasis, p. 110
	extinct, p. 111
grid, p. 106	

Vocabulary Activities Build two word webs for students, using the vocabulary words in the chapter. At the center of one web write the word *maps*. At the center of the second web write the word *climate*. As students read through the unit, have them add vocabulary words to the appropriate web. The webs could be expanded to include geography words. Advise students who have difficulty with the terms to use the glossary.

Before Reading the Chapter Ask students to explain what they already know about globes. Allow students to point out on a globe features with which they are familiar. Review with students the geographic features of your area, such as rivers, mountains, plains, and farmlands. Ask students to describe the climate in your area.

Teaching Suggestions and Answers
Page 105

Ask students if the United States is in the Northern or Southern Hemisphere. (the Northern Hemisphere) **Students should circle the United States on the map. They should answer that the United States is in the Western Hemisphere.**

Page 106

Ask students to name the coordinates for the city of Philadelphia, giving the latitude first. (40°N, 75°W) Then give students the coordinates for cities other than Memphis and Philadelphia. Have them find these places on maps or globes you have in your classroom. **Students should answer that Memphis is at 35°N, 90°W. Students should answer that London is at the 0° meridian, or the Prime Meridian.**

Page 107

Have students locate the area of the North European Plain on the land region map on pages 16–17. **For the first question, students should answer that people would want to live in an area with good farmland so they can grow crops to feed themselves and their families. For the second question, students might suggest that the nearness of the ocean and sea shaped European civilization because chances for trade and contact with other civilizations increase if a civilization is located near a large body of water.**

Page 108

Discuss the fact that Russia is famous for its long, cold winters. Explain that Russia has every kind of climate except tropical, but that it is generally colder than other parts of Europe. Point out that Russia does not enjoy the benefits of the Gulf Stream. **Students should circle Vladivostok, which is in southeast Russia.**

Page 109

Point out that climbing Mount Everest posed a challenge to people for many years. Mountain climbers didn't reach the top until less than 50 years ago. Point out that many rivers start in mountains because tall mountains are often covered with snow. When the snow melts at certain times during the year, streams form that later turn into rivers. Tell students that although farmers depend on the monsoons to bring rain, the rains can often be very heavy and have caused disastrous floods in countries such as India, Bangladesh, and Myanmar. **Students should answer that it is a good name because the Himalaya Mountains have some of the highest peaks in the world.**

Page 110

Discuss with students some of the things that people might have to do in order to live in the desert. (learning how to find and conserve water and how to irrigate fields) Discuss the fact that different types of erosion take place all over the world. **Students might answer that the wind makes shapes in the sand that look like waves. Also, the desert is enormous, like an ocean.**

Project Tip

Help students carry out the suggestion on page 110. You might show students pictures of the kinds of clothing worn by desert tribes. Discuss with them why people who live in the Sahara tend to wear layers of robes rather than skimpy clothing.

Page 111

Have students describe any African animals they have seen in zoos or in pictures. Call on volunteers to describe the animals. Point out that hunters, called poachers, still hunt some animals in Africa, even though it is against the law. They usually hunt elephants because their tusks are made of ivory, which can be sold to other countries. In order to protect the elephants, many countries around the world now refuse to buy ivory. Ask a group of interested students to compile a list of endangered species. Have them find out the reasons why the animals are endangered. **Students should answer that Africa's animals are a valuable resource because many people come to Africa to see the animals, which helps the economy of Africa.**

Page 112

Chapter Checkup You may want to work through the Chapter Checkup with students.

Answers: 1. b **2.** a **3.** d **4.** b **5.** d **6.** c
Students should mention that the geography of South Asia includes mountains, rich plains, and fertile valleys, while much of North Africa is covered by desert.

After Reading the Chapter

Have students work in cooperative-learning groups to locate places on the globe. Each group should make a list of places and a list of the places' parallels and meridians. Have groups exchange their lists of coordinates with each other. Students should use the coordinates to find place names. Groups should verify their answers with one another.

Geography

Have students use maps to compare both the geographical features and climate of the United States with those of Russia.

Writing

Have students research the animals in Africa that are currently in danger of becoming extinct in the wild, such as the elephant and the cheetah. Have each student choose one animal and write a short report on its current status.

History

Have interested students research Sir Edmund Hillary's climb to the top of Mt. Everest. Then have students present the information to the class in the form of a news report.

Chapter Summary World War II ended in Europe in May 1945. Following the war, the Soviet Union was the strongest European nation. Communism, the form of government of the Soviet Union and many Eastern European countries, continued in the region until the early 1990s.

Chapter Objectives Students will learn to

• identify Stalin and the spread of communism in Eastern Europe, as well as the events that led to the Cold War.

• locate Eastern European nations, France, Great Britain, and Germany on a map.

• identify the origins of the Berlin Wall and Gorbachev's role in its elimination.

• identify events which led to the end of the Cold War.

• identify conditions in Russia today.

Vocabulary

diplomats, p. 113	union, p. 117
communism, p. 114	strike, p. 117
blocs, p. 115	glasnost, p. 118
Cold War, p. 115	perestroika, p. 120

Vocabulary Activities Write the words *Cold War* on the chalkboard. Tell students that the term *Cold War* first came into use in 1945. It was used to describe the mistrust between the United States and the Soviet Union. Although the two nations disagreed politically, they chose not to go to war with each other. Have students start a word web with the term *Cold War.* Tell them that as they read, they should add other vocabulary words to the web. Have them explain how the words relate to the Cold War. Encourage students who have difficulty with the terms to use the glossary.

Before Reading the Chapter Ask students to tell what they know about the United Nations. If any students have visited the United Nations building in New York City, ask them to describe their visit to the class. Then, on the chalkboard, create an organizational chart of the United Nations showing its various branches or departments.

Teaching Suggestions and Answers

Page 113

Answers might include relief efforts and disaster aid as ways in which nations might help one another.

Page 114

Ask students to look at the map on this page and locate the nations of France, Great Britain, and Italy on the map. Point out that after World War II, the nations of Eastern Europe lay between these nations and what at that time was the Soviet Union. Stalin wanted to keep the nations of Eastern Europe communist to prevent the West—particularly Germany—from invading the Soviet Union. **Students should circle Finland, Poland, Czechoslovakia, Hungary, and Romania.**

Page 115

Have students name two reasons why 1948 was a dangerous year in Europe. (Germany was divided into two nations—one democratic and one communist. By 1948, communist governments also ruled in Poland, Czechoslovakia, Bulgaria, Romania, Hungary, Albania, and Yugoslavia.) **Students should answer that France and Great Britain belonged to the western bloc.**

Project Tip
Help students carry out the suggestion on page 115. You might direct them to encyclopedia articles and books that will provide them with additional information about various countries and their leaders.

Page 116

Discuss with students why many of the nations of Eastern Europe turned against their communist leaders. (Compared to the nations of Western Europe, the nations of Eastern Europe were poor. The people were not able to choose their own leaders.) **Students should answer that East Germany built the Berlin Wall to keep people from leaving the country.**

Page 117

Point out that in 1983 Lech Walesa won the Nobel Prize for Peace for his efforts to prevent violence while trying to gain workers' rights. Discuss with students why most people think it is important for people in a country to be able to choose their own leaders. **Students should answer that workers in Poland formed a special union because they wanted higher pay and free elections.**

Page 118

Point out that what was once communist Yugoslavia is now the nations of Slovenia, Croatia, Bosnia-Hercegovina, Macedonia, and Yugoslavia. Point out that communist dictatorships had held different groups together by force in Yugoslavia and in the Soviet Union. Disputes and fighting continue among various ethnic groups and nationalities in Eastern Europe and the former Soviet Union. **Students should circle Russia, Kazakhstan, and Ukraine. Students should answer that the Soviet people ended communism because they were poor and wanted more freedom.**

Page 119

You might want to use newspapers and news magazines to update students on current events and the latest developments in Russia. Mention to students that although Russia has had economic and other problems since the fall of communism and a change to a more democratic capitalist government, voters chose to continue to reject communism in July 1996. They reelected Boris Yeltsin as president in a run-off election between Yeltsin and the communist candidate. **Students should answer that among the most important changes that have occurred in Russia following the fall of communism are economic and political changes.**

Page 120

Ask students if they think Gorbachev was a good leader. Point out that under the old Soviet system, people could belong to only one political party—the Communist party. The Communist party nominated all the candidates for elections. Thus, in an election year, only one person ran for each office. Now people in Russia, Ukraine, and other nations once part of the Soviet Union have a chance to vote from among a number of candidates in free elections. **Students should answer that after 1986 people were allowed to own some businesses and farms.**

Page 121

Students should answer that the Chunnel connects England and France.

Page 122

Chapter Checkup You may want to work through the Chapter Checkup with students.

Answers: 1. a **2.** c **3.** c **4.** b **5.** d **6.** c The Cold War cost the Soviet Union a lot of money. Gorbachev hoped to improve the Soviet economy.

After Reading the Chapter

Have students work in groups to find current newspaper and magazine stories and pictures about Russia, Ukraine, or other nations of Eastern Europe. Have them use their clippings to make a bulletin-board display called "Recent Developments in . . . "

History

Ask students to find additional information about Harry Truman and Joseph Stalin in an encyclopedia or a library book. Then have them report their findings to the class.

Geography

Discuss the breakup of the Soviet Union into 15 separate nations. Have students create a bulletin-board display featuring information about conflicts between ethnic groups and nationalities in these nations.

Writing

Have students give a news-broadcast profile of Boris Yeltsin or another Russian political party leader. They can use material from news magazines to write their two- or three-paragraph profiles. You might ask volunteers to read their profiles to the class.

Chapter Summary During the 1300s and 1400s, European explorers and traders told of great resources in Africa. Soon other Europeans came to Africa to start colonies and profit from the continent's wealth. The slave trade was started soon after. Most Africans lived under European rule until after World War II.

Chapter Objectives Students will learn to

- identify the causes and effects of the African slave trade.

- identify European imperialism and its effects on Africa.

- identify the independence movements in African nations.

- locate on maps countries of colonial Africa and of modern Africa.

Vocabulary	
independence, p. 123	imperialism, p. 126
	boycotts, p. 128
plantations, p. 124	apartheid, p. 129
racism, p. 125	

Vocabulary Activities Write the following on the chalkboard: *racism—apartheid.* Explain that racism is the belief that some people are better than others. This belief led, in the country of South Africa, to a system called apartheid, where blacks were forced to live apart from whites. Tell students that, as they read the chapter, they will be able to make a similar diagram using the words *boycotts* and *independence.* Elicit the meanings of the root words for the vocabulary words *imperialism* and *independence: empire* and *depend.* Then give students the two vocabulary words in a sentence, and have them determine their meanings. Remind students who have difficulty with the terms to use the glossary.

Before Reading the Chapter Ask students to discuss what they know about the practice of slavery in North America during the 1700s and 1800s. How did the slaves get here? What work did they do? Have students preview the map on page 127. Ask them to remember what they read about the ancient civilizations of Africa in Chapter 7. Have students find the countries where these civilizations were located by referring to the map on page 60.

Teaching Suggestions and Answers
Page 123

Point out that the European nation that first began long voyages of exploration was Portugal. By the 1400s, Portuguese explorers were the most experienced navigators and sailors in the world. **Students should answer that Europeans found out about the resources of Africa from explorers and traders who brought the news back to Europe.**

Page 124

Direct students' attention to the picture on this page. Ask them how they think European slave traders were able to take so many slaves by force from Africa. (Answers will vary.) **Students should answer that Egypt and Greece had slaves.**

Page 125

Spanish explorers and colonists in the Americas first tried to use American Indians as slaves. Yet the Spaniards found that American Indians often escaped from slavery, returning to their homes in the wilderness. African slaves were not able to escape as easily, since they were in a foreign land and were not as familiar with the surroundings. Ask students to name the causes of the slave trade. Record students' responses on the Cause and Effect graphic organizer found on page 64 of this guide. Then have students name the effects of the slave trade. **Answers may include sickness, and a lack of food and clean air and water.**

Page 126

Point out that by the late 1800s, Great Britain had the world's largest empire. In fact, it was the largest empire that the world had ever known, greater even than the Roman Empire. About one fourth of the world's land and people lived under British rule. Ask students to name two independent countries in Africa in 1951. (Libya, Egypt, Ethiopia, Liberia, Union of South Africa, Southwest Africa) **Answers should include France, Great Britain, Portugal, Belgium, and Spain.**

Page 127

Ask students what nation in Africa today was formerly called the Belgian Congo. (Zaire) **Answers should include Chad, Central African Republic, Gabon, and Congo.**

Page 128

Point out that in the early 1980s one of the worst droughts in history struck Africa. Thousands of people died when crops failed in countries such as Sudan and Ethiopia. **Students should answer that the people of Ghana boycotted the European governments.**

Project Tip

Help students carry out the suggestion on page 128. For example, you might bring recordings of African music to class so students can learn about the music of various cultures in Africa.

Page 129

Explain that political prisoners are people who are imprisoned for their political beliefs. During his time in prison from 1964 to 1990, Nelson Mandela was one of the world's most famous political prisoners. Yet he continued to have a great influence on South Africa, even while in prison. Two South African presidents visited him in jail. South African officials often offered to free Mandela if he would change his views about his struggle for full civil rights for black South Africans. Mandela always refused. Have interested students investigate events in South Africa since the end of apartheid. **Students' answers should include that black people could not go to the same restaurants or schools as whites.**

Page 130

Chapter Checkup Make sure all students understand what the correct answers are to the numbered questions.

Answers: 1. b **2.** b **3.** a **4.** c **5.** c **6.** d
Answers should include that they wanted African resources to trade; they also wanted slaves.

After Reading the Chapter

Work with students to create a time line or use the Sequencing graphic organizer found on page 63 of this guide to show important dates in African history as discussed in the text.

Time Lines

Have cooperative-learning groups research African countries not directly covered in the text. Have them do time lines of the country's history and how it achieved its independence from Europe (or how it was able to remain independent), and what life is like there today.

Writing

Have students write a couple of paragraphs about the places in Africa they would like to visit. What sights would they like to see? Would they want to go on a photographic safari? Volunteers might read their essays to the class.

History

Have students do research and report on South Africans other than Nelson Mandela who worked to end apartheid and win civil rights for all citizens. Possibilities include Steve Biko, Donald Woods, Bishop Desmond Tutu, and Albert John Luthuli.

Chapter Summary The Middle East is an area that is located between three continents. Europe, Asia, and Africa all come together at the eastern end of the Mediterranean Sea. Most people who live in the Middle East are Muslims. The Islamic faith has shaped much of the culture of the Middle East. Most of the world's oil resources are located in the Middle East. Oil plays a major role in the economies of many Middle Eastern countries.

Chapter Objectives Students will learn to

- locate the countries of the Middle East on a map.

- identify Muhammad as the founder of Islam.

- identify the five religious duties, or Pillars, of Islam.

- identify the extended family as the basis of Islamic culture.

- describe the role of oil in the economy of the Middle East.

Vocabulary

nomads, p. 131	fasting, p. 134
Islam, p. 132	pilgrimage, p. 134
faith, p. 133	extended family, p. 135
prayer, p. 133	
alms, p. 134	petroleum, p. 136

Vocabulary Activities Write the word *Islam* on the chalkboard. Then write the words *faith, prayer, alms, fasting,* and *pilgrimage.* Ask students to explain what the pillars of a building do. Guide students to understand that, like the pillars of a building, the five pillars of Islam are the underlying support of the religion of Islam. Tell students that as they read the chapter they will learn more about the religion of Islam. Remind students who have difficulty with any of the terms to use the glossary.

Before Reading the Chapter Have students preview the map on page 132. Have them locate three regions they studied in Unit 2—the ancient civilizations of Mesopotamia, Egypt, and Canaan. Ask students what these regions are called today. Have students identify two major world religions they have read about that began in the Middle East. Explain that in this chapter they will read about the beginnings of another major religion that is followed today by most people in the Middle East.

Teaching Suggestions and Answers

Page 131

Point out that the ancient nomads of the Middle East generally spent the summer camped near wells or streams. The rest of the year was spent traveling over the desert. They used camels to carry their goods, and their homes were usually tents made of goat and camel hair. **Answers to the first question should include four of the following: Egypt, Sudan, Israel, Turkey, Syria, Iraq, Iran, Jordan, Kuwait, as well as other countries in the Middle East. For the second question, students should answer that the distance between Cairo and Jerusalem is about 300 miles.**

Page 132

Point out that during Muhammad's lifetime the Arabs were separated into many different tribes. These tribes often fought against one another. Muhammad and other early Islamic leaders tried to bring the different tribes together. One way they did this was to encourage all Arabs to follow the same religion—Islam. **Students should answer that Mecca is located in Saudi Arabia. Mecca is near the Red Sea.**

Page 133

Point out that, according to Islam, the Koran was revealed to Muhammad by Allah (or god) over a period of 20 years. After Muhammad's death, his followers were afraid that Muhammad's teachings would be lost. They carefully gathered the copies of his teachings that people had written down. Then they collected the writings that eventually formed the Koran. **Students should answer that the duty of prayer is shown.**

Page 134

Explain that early followers of Islam also valued the art of bookmaking. In fact, fine books were made in the Middle East long before they were made in Europe. **Answers will vary but might include some comment on the skill and intricacy of the design.**

Page 135

Discuss with students the advantages and disadvantages of living in an extended family. Point out that in extended families more family members are available to provide care for children and other family members. **Students should answer that according to Islamic law, she must wear a black robe in case she is seen by men outside of her family.**

Project Tip

Help students carry out the suggestion on page 135. Students may want to investigate mosques. Mosques range from very simple rooms to large, elaborate buildings. Many share common features. If possible, obtain a variety of pictures of mosques and have students look for the similarities among the different mosques in the photographs. You might also bring additional books to class showing other examples of Islamic art and architecture.

Page 136

Discuss with students what happens when oil prices are high and what effect high prices have on the sale of oil. The members of OPEC include Algeria, Ecuador, Gabon, Indonesia, Iran, Iraq, Kuwait, Libya, Nigeria, Qatar, Saudi Arabia, United Arab Emirates, and Venezuela. **Students should answer that Saudi Arabia produced five million barrels of oil per day in 1989. In 1989, the United States produced more oil; in 1993, Saudi Arabia produced more oil.**

Page 137

Explain that Golda Meir's parents moved her family to the United States when Golda was eight years old. During the 1940s, Golda Meir moved to Israel. She was one of the signers of the Israeli Declaration of Independence. **Answers might include that most people in Israel practice the religion of Judaism; they also have a democratic**

government. Saudi Arabians, on the other hand, practice Islam and are ruled by a king.

Page 138

Chapter Checkup You may want to work through the Chapter Checkup with students.

Answers: 1. d **2.** b **3.** a **4.** c **5.** c **6.** b Answers might include the kind of art they make, fasting during the ninth month of the year, and the five religious duties they must perform, including praying five times a day.

After Reading the Chapter

Review with students the Five Pillars of Islam. Hold a discussion about how the Islamic faith has influenced life in the Middle East.

History

Have students work in cooperative-learning groups to find out more about the Muslim empire. What regions did the Muslims conquer? When did the empire end, and what lasting effects did it have?

Making a Chart

Ask students to find out more about petroleum. Have them make a chart that lists as many products as they can find out about that are made from petroleum.

Writing

Have students write a brief biography of Muhammad. Direct them to encyclopedia articles and books for reference. Tell them to summarize the high points and achievements of his life in three or four paragraphs.

Chapter Summary Asia is the largest continent on Earth. In 1947, India was divided into two nations, India and Pakistan. Marco Polo visited China in the 1270s. The arrival of European traders caused unrest in China. After World War II, China became a communist country. Japan remained isolated from European countries for many years. In the mid-1800s, Japan began building an Asian empire. After World War II, the country was nearly destroyed. Today Japan is an important industrial nation.

Chapter Objectives Students will learn to

- describe how Europe and the United States have influenced India, China, and Japan.

- identify the impact of Gandhi and Nehru on modern India.

- trace the rise of communism in China.

- explain Japan's growth into a major industrial nation.

- explain the economic prosperity of Hong Kong, South Korea, Singapore, and Taiwan.

Vocabulary

nonviolent, p. 141	reforms, p. 145
civil disobedience, p. 141	commune, p. 146
opium, p. 144	archipelago, p. 147
rebels, p. 145	clans, p. 148
poverty, p. 145	discrimination, p. 152

Vocabulary Activities Write the words *clans, rebels, commune,* and *archipelago* on the chalkboard. Ask the class what these words have in common. Inform students that people join or identify with groups, such as *clans* and *rebels.* Some people choose to live together in a group, like a *commune.* An *archipelago* is a group of islands, which may also be home to a group of people as Japan is. Then write the words *reforms, discrimination, poverty,* and *nonviolent* on the chalkboard. Ask volunteers to write sentences using each of these words in the context of

group. Advise students who have difficulty with any of the terms to use the glossary.

Before Reading the Chapter Ask students to review what they learned in Chapter 6 about the early civilizations of China and India. Tell them that in this chapter they will read how China's and India's governments changed after thousands of years.

Teaching Suggestions and Answers

Page 139

Students should answer that Africa also has both deserts and rain forests.

Page 140

Explain that the British set up trading posts in three of India's coastal villages. In time, these villages grew into the major cities of Bombay, Madras, and Calcutta. Have students find these cities on the map on page 141. **Answers could include that the British wanted to control India's resources and ports.**

Page 141

Mention that in 1947 Pakistan consisted of East and West Pakistan, which today are Bangladesh and Pakistan, respectively. Have students locate Pakistan on the map. **Students should underline New Delhi as the capital of India and circle Islamabad as the capital of Pakistan.**

Page 142

Answers might include population growth, as well as religious and political violence.

Page 143

Europeans who read about Marco Polo's travels at first thought that they must be exaggerations. Few Europeans had imagined that such an advanced civilization existed in Asia. **Students should mark an X on Manchuria, which is northeast of Beijing.**

Page 144

Students should answer that Japan is about 700 miles from the island of Taiwan.

Page 145

Discuss with students why it would have been difficult for the Nationalists to find the Communists once they had escaped into the mountains. (Mountains are difficult to cross, and they offer many hiding places.) **Students should answer that rule by emperors ended in China in 1912, and that the Communists took control of China in 1949.**

Page 146

Answers might include that the people in China have some economic freedoms, but few political freedoms.

Page 147

Explain that the Japanese archipelago is actually a mountain range rising from the ocean floor. Some of the mountains are volcanoes. **Students should answer that four large islands make up the Japanese archipelago and that Tokyo is located at 140°E line of longitude.**

Page 148

Ask students to identify the names of the four major islands that make up the nation of Japan. (Honshu, Hokkaido, Kyushu, and Shikoku) **Students should circle the Sea of Japan.**

Page 149

Point out that Perry's ships were made out of iron and were much larger than the Japanese ships at this time. Ask: Why do you think the Japanese were willing to trade after years of isolation? (Because they were impressed with Perry's show of strength.) **Students should answer that after World War II, Japan was nearly destroyed; the Japanese rebuilt their factories; they produced consumer goods such as cars, televisions, and cameras.**

Project Tip

Help students carry out the suggestion on page 149. If possible, bring menus from Indian, Chinese, or Japanese restaurants to class. Students can use these menus to create a sample dinner menu.

Page 150

Students should answer that in 1984, 18 percent of Japan's leading electronic products were videocassette recorders; in 1994, they were 24 percent. Japan's production of electronic products between 1984 and 1994 increased from 66 million to 1 billion.

Page 151

Explain to students that the Korean peninsula is made up of North Korea and South Korea. North Korea has been a communist country since 1945. South Korea has a democratic government. **Students should answer that the "four little tigers" are alike in that they all have strong and successful economies.**

Page 152

Special People Point out that in our country, Dr. Martin Luther King, Jr., and César Chávez were influenced by Gandhi's ideas of nonviolence. **Students should answer that discrimination in South Africa influenced Gandhi to work for human rights.**

Page 153

Chapter Checkup You may want to work through the Chapter Checkup with students.

Answers: 1. b **2.** c **3.** a **4.** b **5.** c **6.** d Answers will vary. Some examples might include the growth of factories, the use of technology, the improvement of methods adopted from the West, the growing markets for electronic goods.

After Reading the Chapter

Review with students the changes that have taken place in India, China, and Japan. Ask students to explain why these changes are good or bad.

Art

Students can work in cooperative-learning groups to make relief maps of parts of the Eastern Hemisphere. They can use clay, plaster of Paris, or another medium to show physical features such as Mount Fuji, the Himalaya mountain range, and the Ganges River.

Writing

Have students work in groups. Allow them to choose a person discussed in Chapter 16. Then have them research and write a report about the person and present their findings to the class.

Chapter Summary Australia, New Zealand, and the islands of the South Pacific make up Oceania. The native peoples of Oceania were expert sailors. Dutch explorers came to Oceania in 1606. European settlers followed soon after. Today, Australia is one of the richest countries in the world. Many people in New Zealand work on modern farms. Fishing is also an important part of the economy. People that live on some of the smaller islands of Oceania live much the way people have lived there for centuries.

Chapter Objectives Students will learn to

- identify Oceania as an area in the southern Pacific Ocean made up of Australia, New Zealand, and thousands of islands.

- recount Australian history from the time of the early Aborigines to the present.

- recount the history of New Zealand from the time of the early Maori to the present.

- locate features of Australia and New Zealand on a map.

Vocabulary

outback, p. 155	Maori, p. 157
Aborigines, p. 156	convicts, p. 158
boomerang, p. 156	polyps, p. 160

Vocabulary Activities Make separate word webs for *Australia* and *New Zealand*. Explain that the Aborigines were the first people to live in Australia and add their name to the web. Do the same with the Maori of New Zealand. As students read the chapter, have them add words to each of the webs.

Before Reading the Chapter Ask students to discuss what they already know about Australia and New Zealand. Ask if anyone has seen or touched coral from the sea. Encourage students to relate what they know about coral and about how it is formed. On a globe or a map, point out the area of the southern Pacific Ocean. Show students where Australia and New Zealand are located.

Teaching Suggestions and Answers
Page 154
You may wish to point out the countries of Oceania on a globe. Mention to students that Sydney has been chosen as the site of the summer Olympic games in the year 2000. **Students should answer that Sydney looks like a modern, new city.**

Page 155
Point out to students that one reason Australia is sometimes referred to as the "Land Down Under" is that it lies completely south of the Equator. Have students locate the Great Barrier Reef. (It is located off the northeast coast of Australia.) **Students should answer that the capital city of Australia is Canberra and the capital of New Zealand is Wellington. When it is 10 P.M. in Sydney, it is noon in London.**

Page 156
Point out that, in the twentieth century, the Aborigines have gone through a period of great change. Many have left the desert and gone to work on cattle stations and sheep ranches. There the Aborigines work for money to buy food and other things that they need. Other Aborigines have moved to Australia's big cities. Very few Aborigines today live as nomads in the desert. **Students should answer that the wooden dish of the Aborigines is called a coolamon.**

Page 157
One way in which the Maori were different from the Aborigines of Australia was that they knew how to build and travel in large canoes. Discuss with students why people on small islands might be more likely to learn how to travel by boat. (The sea is part of their natural environment; they may need to travel to other islands to get what they need.) **Students should answer that the Maori fished in the Pacific Ocean.**

Page 158
Explain that, at first, the British were not interested in Australia. They thought it was too far away. After they lost their colonies in the United

States in 1783, however, they began to look at Australia as a place where they could send convicts, or prisoners. Before the American Revolution, the British had sent some convicts to the American colonies, but the number was insignificant in comparison with the number they would later send to Australia. **Students should circle Tasmania and the Tasman Sea on the map on page 155.**

Project Tip

Help students carry out the suggestion on page 158. For example, you might display to the class a globe of the world. Locate for them the vast area covered by Oceania. While looking at the globe, have them speculate on how the interplay between island and ocean has affected people's lives in Oceania.

Page 159

Point out that, for centuries, life on most small Pacific Islands centered around the sea. Fishing provided most of the food for island peoples. This was especially true for small islands that did not have good soil for growing crops. Even today, the sea is important to Pacific Islanders. People from the Pacific Islands are excellent sailors, and many young people take jobs on large ships and sail throughout the world. **Students should answer that New Zealand became a nation in 1907.**

Page 160

For Your Information Explain that coral reefs are found in warm climates, because the tiny polyps that form coral cannot live in cold water. Point out that coral reefs can be found in the United States off the coast of Florida. **Students should answer that the Great Barrier Reef is located in the Coral Sea.**

Page 161

Chapter Checkup To make sure all students understand the correct answers, you may want to work through the Chapter Checkup with students.

Answers: 1. c **2.** d **3.** b **4.** a **5.** d **6.** a
The Maori grew crops and, instead of moving from place to place, built houses out of reeds. The Aborigines hunted and gathered their food. They did not farm or build villages.

After Reading the Chapter

Science

Using the Great Barrier Reef as a starting point, have students make a bulletin-board display about the natural wonders of Australia. Have students look through magazines and travel brochures for pictures of natural formations such as Ayers Rock and for unusual wildlife such as kangaroos and koalas.

Geography

Students might make a chart or bulletin-board display about the shipping and fishing industries, showing the various types of crafts used in different countries throughout history, from Japan to Great Britain to New Zealand.

Writing

Have students work in cooperative-learning groups to research the islands that make up Melanesia, Micronesia, and Polynesia. Have each group use encyclopedias and other library resources to investigate one of the following topics: language, religion, village and town life, arts and crafts, or climate and geography. Then have a "Pacific Islands" day on which students present their reports to the class.

Art

Inform students that the Maori considered wood carving a sacred activity because of the images of power that were created. You may wish to bring to class some books on Maori art to give students an idea of the kind of images they created. Have students draw their own idea of a powerful image. It could be in the Maori style or something original. Students may also wish to include a paragraph that explains the concept.

Unit Summary Geographic features that both the North and South American continents have in common include the Rockies and Andes mountains in the west, and the plains in the interior of each continent. American and Canadian history ranges from early American Indian culture to European settlement and domination, followed by independence from Great Britain. The countries of Latin America fought for many years before gaining independence from Spain, Portugal, and France.

Before Reading the Unit Introduce the unit by asking students to identify the Western Hemisphere on a globe or map. (You may wish to use the map of the Eastern and Western Hemispheres on page 105.) Encourage students to discuss what they know about the Western Hemisphere by asking questions such as: What mountain range runs along the western side of North America? (the Rockies) What mountain range runs along the western side of South America? (the Andes)

Have students open their books to the unit opener on page 164. Encourage students to think about the questions as they read the unit. Point out the Unit Project box to students and explain that they will work on this project as they read through the unit.

Unit Project

Setting Up the Project Brainstorm with the class the things they will need to make the film. Write the items on the chalkboard. Have them add to this list as they read the unit.

Students will find specific suggestions in the Project Tip sections of the chapters. Encourage students to adapt the suggestions to their own interests.

Presenting the Project One alternative possibility might be to make an outline of two or three different possible scenarios for their movie. Making an outline of two or three possibilities will help students decide which would make the better film.

After Reading the Unit Invite discussion of the questions on the unit opener and the answers students discovered about the Western Hemisphere. Check students' understanding of the material by asking some of the following

questions. What are the names of the continents that make up the Western Hemisphere? Where did the explorers of North and South America come from? What are some problems faced by Latin America today?

Skill Builder

Using an Elevation Map

As students read page 192, remind them that elevation means the height of the land above sea level. An elevation map measures in feet or meters the height of mountains, plateaus, plains, and other land regions above sea level.

Answers: **1.** the Coastal Plain **2.** the Rocky Mountains **3.** 3,280–6,560 feet **4.** Answers will vary.

Bibliography

Teacher

Blashfield, Jean. *Galapagos Islands.* (Wonders of the World Series) Raintree Steck-Vaughn, 1995. (Grades 6–7)

Rosen, Susanna van. *The Earth Atlas.* Borling Kindersley, 1995.

Willis, Terri. *St. Lawrence River and Seaway.* (Wonders of the World Series) Raintree Steck-Vaughn, 1995. (Grades 6–7)

Student

Alexander, Bryan and Cherry. *Inuit.* (Threatened Cultures Series) Steck-Vaughn, 1993. (Grades 5–6)

Anderson, Dale. *Explorers Who Found New Worlds.* (20 Events Series) Raintree Steck-Vaughn, 1994. (Grades 5–6)

Chrisp, Peter. *The Spanish Conquests in the New World.* (Exploration and Encounters Series) Thomson Learning, 1993. (Grades 4–6)

Columbus Sails Again! The American History Herald. Steck-Vaughn, 1992. (Grade 5)

Lewington, Anne. *Rain Forest Amerindians.* (Threatened Cultures Series) Steck-Vaughn, 1993. (Grades 5–6)

Teacher's Resource Binder

Blackline Masters for Unit 5: Unit 5 Project Organizer, Unit 5 Review, Unit 5 Test; Activities for Chapters 18, 19, 20; Outline Maps of the World, Hemispheres, North America, South America

Chapter Summary Only two of the seven continents are in the Western Hemisphere—North America and South America. The United States and Canada have many of the same land regions. Panama in Central America is the site of the Panama Canal. The Panama Canal links the Atlantic and Pacific oceans. The mountains of South America are part of the same range that passes through North America. In the United States and Canada, they are called the Rockies. In South America, they are known as the Andes. The Amazon Rain Forest of South America is in danger of being destroyed by people who clear the land for farming.

Chapter Objectives Students will learn to

- locate North and South America on a map.

- identify early European discoverers of the Americas.

- compare the geography and climate of Canada, the United States, Central America, and South America.

Vocabulary

Canadian Shield,   locks, p. 170
    p. 167

fjords, p. 168   Amazon Basin,
    p. 171

canal, p. 169

Vocabulary Activities Review with students some of the landforms they have learned about thus far. As students learn about the new landforms and waterways, have them make illustrations of the new words. Then, attach these student-made illustrations to the appropriate area on a large classroom map.

Before Reading the Chapter Have students preview the pictures of the United States in Chapter 18, and ask what they know about the geography of our country. If any students in the class have lived in another part of the United States, have them describe ways in which that region is different from, or the same as, your area. Ask students to relate what they already know about our

neighbors to the north and south. If students have visited Canada or Latin America, encourage them to describe what they saw. Ask students to describe the tallest mountains they have seen. If anyone has seen both the Rockies and the Appalachians, ask them to compare the two ranges.

Teaching Suggestions and Answers

Page 165

Use a large map to show the seven continents. Ask if anyone has ever noticed how Africa and South America seem to "fit together." Explain that scientists believe that millions of years ago the seven continents all fit together to form one giant continent. **Students will probably recognize North and South America.**

Page 166

Ask students what they might have named these new lands if they had discovered them. You may wish to write their suggestions on the board. **Students should answer that Cabot sailed across the Atlantic Ocean to reach Canada. Students will probably answer that the modern map seems more accurate.**

Page 167

Point out that Canada's capital, Ottawa, is located in southeastern Canada. Tell students they will read more about Canada in Chapter 19. **Students should answer that the west coast of Canada is warmer than the east coast.**

Page 168

Ask students where they would expect to find the coldest temperature in the United States. (Alaska) Where would they find the hottest temperature? (Death Valley in California) **Students should answer that mountains and plains are two land regions that the United States and Canada have in common.**

Project Tip

Help students carry out the suggestion on page 168. For example, you might bring books about Canada and the United States to class and show students pictures of some of the famous scenery.

Page 169

Explain to students that the climate in Central America is warmer than the climate in most of the United States because it is closer to the Equator. **Students should answer that ships had to travel all the way around the continent of South America.**

Page 170

Point out that the Panama Canal was finished in 1914 at a cost of $380 million. Thousands of people worked to cut the canal through jungles, hills, and swamps. **Students should answer that the canal is important because it connects the Atlantic and Pacific oceans.**

Page 171

Tell students that the Amazon is the second-longest river in the world. Only the Nile River in Egypt is longer. Also, point out that about half of all the different plants and animals on Earth live in the tropical rain forests of South America. **Answers should include that both North and South America have mountains in the west and have flat plains regions in the middle of each continent.**

Page 172

Inform students that the rain forests absorb carbon dioxide and provide much of the world's oxygen. Burning the rain forests (the primary method of clearing) creates more carbon dioxide, which adds to the destruction of Earth's ozone layer. As a result, the world receives less protection from the sun's harmful ultraviolet rays. Ultraviolet rays can cause cancer.

Page 173

Have students estimate how many Galapagos tortoises might fit in the classroom. **Students should answer that powerful winds from storms might have brought birds to the islands; some animals might have arrived on trees that floated in ocean currents.**

Page 174

Chapter Checkup You may want to work through the Chapter Checkup with students. Make sure they all understand what the correct answers are to the numbered questions.

Answers: 1. b **2.** d **3.** a **4.** c **5.** d **6.** a
Students' answers will vary, but might include Columbia, Cabotia, Henriana, and so forth.

After Reading the Chapter

Review with students the similarities and differences between North America and South America. Discuss climate and landforms.

Geography

Ask students to use maps or globes to compare the distance across the Panama Canal to the distance around South America. It may be helpful to use a piece of paper or a string for measuring.

Science

Have students study and then report on climate in different cities of the Western Hemisphere. Have students follow for two or three weeks newspaper accounts of weather patterns in selected cities, and then have them compare temperature and other conditions. You may wish to post the information on a bulletin board.

Writing

Have students write a dialogue between John Cabot and King Henry VII. The dialogue should bring out the contrast between what Cabot thought he would find in Canada and what he actually found. Students might work in small groups to write their dialogues.

Science

Have interested students find out more about the wildlife of the Amazon Rain Forest. Suggest that students choose animals such as three-toed sloths, capybaras (the world's largest rodents), howler monkeys, arrow poison frogs, boa constrictors, flesh-eating piranhas, titan beetles (that can grow to be six inches long), or other animals they find intriguing. Ask students to discover why the habitat of the rain forest is suitable for the animal they studied. Students may also gather information about the animal's eating habits and the sounds or calls the animal makes. Have students share their findings with the class.

Chapter Summary Explorers from Europe reached Canada between the years 1000 and about 1600. English and French people eventually settled in Canada. There were many battles about who should rule Canada. In 1763 the British gained control. In 1867 Canada gained the right to self-government. Today, Canada is home to people from many lands. Canada also has a large population of American Indians, the original inhabitants of Canada.

Chapter Objectives Students will learn to

• compare elevation levels on an elevation map.

• identify the first Europeans in Canada.

• describe the roles of France and Great Britain in Canadian history.

• identify how Canada became an independent nation, and explain the problems and challenges it faces today.

Vocabulary

elevation map,   secede, p. 180
    p. 176

multiculturalism,
    p. 179

Vocabulary Activities Tell students that the prefix *multi* means "many" in Latin. Ask them to review the meaning of the word *culture*. In Canada, multiculturalism refers to a program designed to help people share their different ways of life. Inform students that the word *secede* also has a Latin origin. It comes from the word *secedere;* the Latin *se* means "apart" and *cedere* means "to go." Encourage students to use the glossary if they are having difficulty with any of the terms.

Before Reading the Chapter Ask if any students in the class have visited Canada. If so, have them describe the regions they visited and what they saw on their trip. Ask students what they know about areas in the United States in which more than one language is spoken. Where does this happen? What are some of the effects of having more than one language spoken in an area?

Teaching Suggestions and Answers
Page 175

Refer students to the photograph on this page of Parliament Hill in Ottawa, the seat of Canadian government. Point out that Ottawa, the capital of Canada, is located where three rivers come together. These rivers served as passageways for explorers and traders over several centuries. The name Ottawa is an American Indian name for a tribe that lived in this part of Canada. The city was named the capital of Canada in 1855 by Queen Victoria of Great Britain. **Students should answer that countries that do not have forests would not be able to make buildings out of logs.**

Page 176

Point out that Canada is made up of ten provinces and two territories: Newfoundland, Quebec, Ontario, Manitoba, Saskatchewan, Alberta, British Columbia, Prince Edward Island, Nova Scotia, New Brunswick, Yukon Territory, and Northwest Territories. Ask students to name the province in which the capital of Ottawa is located. (Ontario) **Students should answer that Whitehorse is at an elevation between 2,000 to 4,000 feet.** Ask students if Whitehorse is at a higher or lower elevation than Yellowknife. (Whitehorse is higher than Yellowknife.)

Page 177

Point out that Canada was explored at the same time Europeans were exploring other parts of North and South America. The Spanish and Portuguese primarily explored lands in South America. The French and English were eager to compete with the Spanish and Portuguese. They began exploring and creating settlements in North America. At the time, South America was considered more valuable. It was thought that more gold and silver could be found there. **Students should circle Hudson Bay on the map.**

Page 178

Point out that the railroad proved extremely useful in the wilderness areas of Canada and the United States. Railroads were used to haul almost everything that pioneers needed, such as food, cattle, lumber and other building supplies, and many other goods. New towns quickly grew up along railroad tracks. Sometimes railroad towns began to be built even before the railroad reached them. **Students should answer that they are building a railroad.**

Page 179

Discuss with students why people from so many different places around the world wanted to settle in Canada. (Canada offered more living space. People could build larger farms and find more opportunities in Canada.) **Students should answer that French and English cultures are represented by the writing on the sign.**

Project Tip

Help students answer the question on page 179. For example, you might suggest some event having to do with the Royal Canadian Mounted Police (the Mounties), the fur traders from the Hudson's Bay Company, or perhaps a scenario based on the Gold Rush in the Klondike region in the 1890s.

Page 180

Point out that Canada's province of Quebec is a huge region. All of Great Britain, Ireland, France, Spain, Belgium, the Netherlands, Denmark, and Switzerland would fit into Quebec. Quebec also has many factories, natural resources, and good ports. Have students look at the map on page 176 and name two cities in Quebec. (Montreal and Quebec) **Students should answer that it is cold.**

Page 181

Have students locate the Beaufort Sea on the map on page 176. Point out that many Inuit people today have the freedom to move to other parts of Canada if they wish. However, they often have great problems adapting to life in Canadian cities. Many Inuit have trouble finding jobs. Others miss their traditional way of life. Many Inuit who left their homelands have returned. **Students should answer a seal.**

Page 182

Chapter Checkup You may want to work through the Chapter Checkup with students.

Answers: 1. a **2.** d **3.** c **4.** b **5.** b **6.** d
British and French are major cultures. Most of

the countries of Europe are represented, as well as most of the countries of the world. There is also an important American Indian culture represented by the Inuit, among others.

After Reading the Chapter

Time Lines

Have students work in groups to make time lines that show the history of Canada. They can use the information in their texts, or they may do further research.

Making Bar Graphs

Have students consult a recent almanac to find out the population and land area of each province and territory. Then have students construct two bar graphs, one to rank the provinces and territories by population; the other to rank them by area.

Writing

Have students do some research on one of the following topics: the Hudson's Bay Company, the Klondike Gold Rush of the 1890s, the Royal Canadian Mounted Police. They can find information about these topics in an encyclopedia. Then have them write one or two paragraphs summarizing the information.

Making a Bulletin-Board Display

Students might make a bulletin-board display about the Inuit showing traditional and present-day life: dress, families, dwellings, fishing, and arts and crafts.

Chapter Summary The Maya, Aztecs, and Inca were American Indian groups who settled in Latin America thousands of years ago. People from Europe arrived in Latin America about 500 years ago. Many parts of Latin America became colonies of various European countries. In the 1800s and 1900s many colonies won independence. Today, Latin America is becoming increasingly industrialized. Although industrialization has brought jobs, serious problems such as pollution and overcrowding have resulted.

Chapter Objectives Students will learn to

- describe the impact of various European settlers on Latin America.

- identify from a map various languages spoken in Latin America.

- use a map to compare the dates of independence of Latin American countries.

- recount Latin American history from European conquest to the present time.

Vocabulary

skyscrapers, p. 187

overcrowding, p. 188

industrialization, p. 188

Vocabulary Activities Write the vocabulary word *industrialization* on the chalkboard, and ask students what they think it means. Tell students that industrialization is the change a country makes when its economy changes from farming to making goods in factories. Write *skyscrapers* on the chalkboard and display pictures of skyscrapers. Discuss why the buildings have the name *skyscraper.* Explain how *industrialization* and *skyscrapers* relate to one another. Write the word *overcrowding* on the chalkboard. Ask students what relation overcrowding may have with the other two words. Challenge students to use all three words together in a sentence. Remind students to use the glossary if they are having difficulty with any of the vocabulary words.

Before Reading the Chapter Ask students what they remember about the Maya, Aztecs, and

Inca. You may wish to refer them to Chapter 6, page 57, for review. Explain that in this chapter they will read about what happened in Latin America after Europeans arrived in the Western Hemisphere. Ask students what they know about life in Latin America today. If students have visited any Latin American countries, encourage them to describe what they learned. If any Latin American countries are currently in the local news, discuss the events with the class.

Teaching Suggestions and Answers

Page 183

Point out that Latin America got its name because the earliest colonizers were from countries that spoke Latin-based languages: Spanish, Portuguese, and French. **Students should answer Suriname, Guyana, and French Guiana.**

Page 184

Explain that settlers from other European countries also began to arrive in Latin America in the 1800s. People from Asia started coming to the area to work after slavery was prohibited. Ask students to name the only country in Latin America where Portuguese is spoken. (Brazil) Point out that Brazil is a very large country. About one third of the people in Latin America live there. **Students should list the two main reasons as gold and good farmland.**

Page 185

Discuss with students whether Spain's colonies in Latin America would have been quick to fight for their independence if the American colonies had lost their fight for independence from Great Britain. **Answers might include El Salvador, Costa Rica, or Venezuela.**

Page 186

Ask students how people in the United States honored George Washington, who led the American Army in the war for independence against Great Britain. (The capital of the country, Washington, D.C., was named after him.) **Students should trace the borders of Colombia, Ecuador, Peru, Venezuela, and Bolivia.**

Page 187

Discuss with students the different kinds of buildings that can be found in your area, and whether any new construction is taking place now. Discuss the difference between newer buildings and buildings from 50 or 60 years ago. **Answers will vary but might include New York, Los Angeles, or Chicago.**

Page 188

Point out that the Amazon Rain Forest gets its name from the fact that the Amazon river flows through the middle of the forest. Most of the forest lies in the Latin American country of Brazil. **Students should answer that the air in Mexico City is hard to breathe because it is so polluted.**

Project Tip

Help students answer the question on page 188. For example, you might read to students from a biography of Bolívar. Then ask them to make casting suggestions for actors to play the part of Bolívar.

Page 189

Explain to students that a government order forbidding trade with another country is called an *embargo*. **Students should answer that the name of the communist dictator of Cuba is Fidel Castro.**

Page 190

Point out that Gabriela Mistral's real name was Lucila Godoy Alcayaga. Explain that the poetry of Gabriela Mistral (1889–1957) is sad and often intense. Her best-known books are *Tala* and *Desolation*. **Students should say that she was a schoolteacher who served on cultural committees at the United Nations.**

Page 191

Chapter Checkup To make sure all students understand the answers to the numbered questions, work through the Chapter Checkup with students.

Answers: 1. c **2.** b **3.** d **4.** d **5.** a **6.** a
Answers may include keeping his army together, finding new soldiers, finding food, and getting supplies.

After Reading the Chapter

Work with students to make a bulletin-board display about the three cultures of Latin America. Help them look in magazines and travel brochures for photographs of Indian and Spanish art and architecture, as well as examples of modern Latin American art.

Writing

Ask students to work in groups to find out more about a topic of interest in this chapter. Possible topics could include life in Mexico City, the Amazon Rain Forest, or Simón Bolívar and the fight for independence. Ask each group to write a report on the topic they chose.

Language Arts

Have students write a poem about someone or something they have read about in this chapter. The subjects of their poems might include Fidel Castro, Simón Bolívar, Gabriela Mistral, the rain forest and its preservation, independence, and so on.

Music

Have students work in groups to learn about the music of one or two cultures from Latin America. Students who play a musical instrument might play for the class. Students might also bring in recordings to share.

Final Test

The final test on the following three pages covers material from the entire book, with emphasis on material from Units 4 and 5, Chapters 12–20.

Answers: 1. b **2.** a **3.** d **4.** c **5.** a **6.** b **7.** c **8.** d **9.** c **10.** a **11.** b **12.** c **13.** d **14.** c **15.** a **16.** b **17.** a **18.** c **19.** d **20.** a **21.** b **22.** d **23.** c **24.** b **25.** a **26.** b **27.** d **28.** c **29.** a **30.** b

Final Test

Complete each sentence. Circle the letter in front of the correct answer.

1. To meet their many needs, people form groups called
   - **a.** languages.
   - **b.** communities.
   - **c.** governments.
   - **d.** economies.

2. Mountains, highlands, plateaus, and plains are four main types of
   - **a.** land regions.
   - **b.** climate regions.
   - **c.** populations.
   - **d.** precipitation.

3. All the things that people use to meet their needs are called
   - **a.** minerals.
   - **b.** pollution.
   - **c.** conservation.
   - **d.** resources.

4. The people of Sumer created the first civilization in
   - **a.** Egypt.
   - **b.** Africa.
   - **c.** Mesopotamia.
   - **d.** Rome.

5. The longest river in the world is the
   - **a.** Nile.
   - **b.** Huang He.
   - **c.** Indus.
   - **d.** Niger.

6. The kingdoms of Kush and Axum were in
   - **a.** Timbuktu.
   - **b.** Ancient Africa.
   - **c.** Ancient Egypt.
   - **d.** Sumer.

7. A form of government invented in Athens was
   - **a.** dictatorship.
   - **b.** monarchy.
   - **c.** democracy.
   - **d.** military rule.

8. The teachings of Jesus were part of a new religion called
   - **a.** Pax Romana.
   - **b.** Judaism.
   - **c.** Anno Domini.
   - **d.** Christianity.

9. The followers of Islam are known as
   - **a.** Christians.
   - **b.** Jews.
   - **c.** Muslims.
   - **d.** Hindus.

10. The Reformation was led by a German monk named
    - **a.** Martin Luther.
    - **b.** Francesco Petrarch.
    - **c.** Leonardo da Vinci.
    - **d.** William the Conqueror.

Final Test (continued)

11. The world is divided into the Eastern and Western Hemispheres by the

    a. Equator.
    b. Prime Meridian.
    c. grid.
    d. lines of latitude.

12. Special winds that affect the climate of South Asia are called

    a. latitudes.
    b. grids.
    c. monsoons.
    d. hemispheres.

13. In order to keep East Germans from escaping to West Germany, the Communists built the

    a. United Nations.
    b. Cold War.
    c. Soviet bloc.
    d. Berlin Wall.

14. In 1981, Poland's workers formed a union called

    a. Glasnost.
    b. Perestroika.
    c. Solidarity.
    d. Chunnel.

15. The belief that people of some races are better than people of other races is called

    a. racism.
    b. independence.
    c. imperialism.
    d. boycotts.

16. When people refuse to buy goods produced by another group, their action is called

    a. a strike.
    b. a boycott.
    c. glasnost.
    d. a union.

17. People who move from place to place in search of food and water are called

    a. nomads.
    b. Arabs.
    c. Muslims.
    d. farmers.

18. The Koran is the holy book of

    a. Christianity.
    b. Judaism.
    c. Islam.
    d. Hinduism.

19. Peacefully breaking unfair laws as a means of protest is called

    a. communism.
    b. industrialization.
    c. discrimination.
    d. civil disobedience.

20. The leader of China during the Great Leap Forward in the 1950s was

    a. Mao Zedong.
    b. Mohandas Gandhi.
    c. Jawaharlal Nehru.
    d. Marco Polo.

Final Test (continued)

21. Australia's hot, dry plains are known as the

    a. archipelago.
    b. outback.
    c. Oceania.
    d. Sahara.

22. Polynesia, Micronesia, and Melanesia are the three main groups of islands that make up

    a. New Zealand.
    b. Hawaii.
    c. Australia.
    d. Oceania.

23. The first name of the Italian explorer Vespucci gave us the name for

    a. Canada.
    b. Mexico.
    c. America.
    d. Panama.

24. Along the western edge of South America run the

    a. Rocky Mountains.
    b. Andes Mountains.
    c. Appalachian Mountains.
    d. Himalaya Mountains.

25. In order to connect the Atlantic Ocean to the Pacific Ocean, American engineers built a

    a. canal.
    b. bridge.
    c. tunnel.
    d. highway.

26. The first Europeans to visit Canada were the

    a. British.
    b. Vikings.
    c. French.
    d. Italians.

27. The fur trade in the huge region of northern Canada was controlled by the

    a. Vikings.
    b. French.
    c. Spanish.
    d. Hudson's Bay Company.

28. Most of Latin America was ruled by the

    a. British.
    b. Dutch.
    c. Spanish.
    d. French.

29. The people of South America were led in their war of independence by

    a. Simón Bolívar.
    b. Christopher Columbus.
    c. John Cabot.
    d. Jacques Cartier.

30. The communist dictator of Cuba is

    a. Gabriela Mistral.
    b. Fidel Castro.
    c. Simón Bolívar.
    d. John Cabot.

Letter to Families

Dear Family:

Throughout this school year, your child will be studying world civilizations, cultures, and geographical regions by using the book *World Cultures Past and Present*. In the five units, your child will learn how geography, trade, and technology affect a civilization's development and the growth of its culture. Your child will also learn how different world economies and governments affect one another. Your child will learn about civilizations of long ago and of today and how they are similar and different.

You can help your child reinforce what we study. Encourage him or her to talk to you about what we are doing. You might even want to ask your child to read aloud for you a page or two of the book or to show you some of the pictures and maps.

Listed below are a number of additional activities you might want to consider doing with your child to support our study of the book.

Thank you for your interest and support.

Sincerely,

_____

World Traveling

Ask your child to choose a country that he or she would like to visit. Discuss why that country is of interest. Locate the country on a globe or world map. Then trace a route to the country. How could you get there? What continents, bodies of water, and countries would you cross on your journey?

Folkways

At the public library find folktales to read with your child. Which tales are similar to stories that your child already knows?

Label Hunt

What products do you use that come from other countries? Look at labels on clothing, food packages, utensils, and machinery.

Museum Trip

Visit a local museum that offers exhibits on another culture or era. Take notes on your impressions and observations.

Recipes

Help your child find a recipe that comes from or that includes a food from another culture. Prepare the recipe together.

Carta a las Familias

Fecha _____

Estimada familia:

Durante este año escolar, su hijo o hija usará el libro *World Cultures Past and Present* para estudiar las civilizaciones, las culturas y las regiones geográficas del mundo. En las cinco unidades del libro su hijo o hija aprenderá cómo la geografía, el comercio y la tecnología afectan al desarrollo de una civilización y el crecimiento de su cultura. También aprenderá cómo las distintas economías y gobiernos del mundo se afectan los unos a los otros, acerca de las civilizaciones antiguas y modernas, y las diferencias y similitudes entre dichas civilizaciones.

Usted puede ayudar a su hijo o hija a reforzar en casa lo que estamos estudiando en la escuela. Para hacerlo, anímelo a conversar sobre lo que estamos haciendo. Puede incluso pedirle que le lea en voz alta una o dos páginas del libro o que le enseñe algunos de los dibujos y los mapas que aparecen en el libro.

A continuación usted encontrará varias actividades adicionales que puede hacer con su hijo o hija para apoyar nuestros estudios.

Muchas gracias por su interés y su apoyo.

Atentamente,

_____

Viaja por el mundo

Pídale a su hijo o hija que escoja un país que le gustaría visitar. Conversen sobre su interés en ese país. Busque el país en un globo o mapa. Luego trace una ruta para llegar a ese país. ¿Cómo pueden llegar hasta allí? ¿Qué continentes, masas de agua y países cruzarían en su viaje?

Costumbres tradicionales

Busque en la biblioteca pública cuentos tradicionales para leerlos con su hijo o hija. ¿Qué cuentos son parecidos a los cuentos que su hijo o hija ya conoce?

En busca de etiquetas

¿Qué productos usan en su casa que provienen de otros países? Busquen etiquetas en vestidos, paquetes de alimentos, utensilios y máquinas.

Un viaje al museo

Visiten un museo local que tenga exhibiciones de otra cultura o de otra época. Tomen notas de sus impresiones y observaciones.

Recetas

Ayude a su hijo o hija a encontrar una receta que provenga de otra cultura o que incluya un alimento de otra cultura. Preparen juntos la receta.

Name _____

Concept Web

Name _____

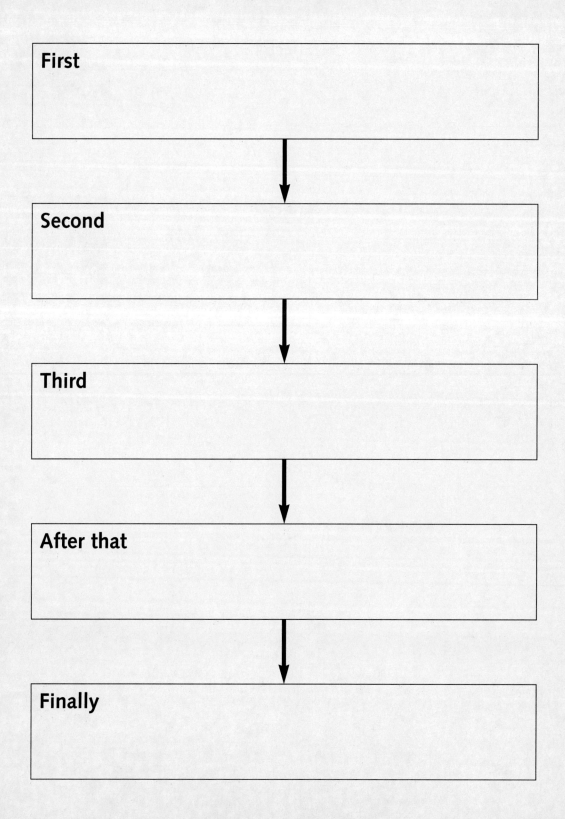

First

↓

Second

↓

Third

↓

After that

↓

Finally

Name _____

Cause and Effect

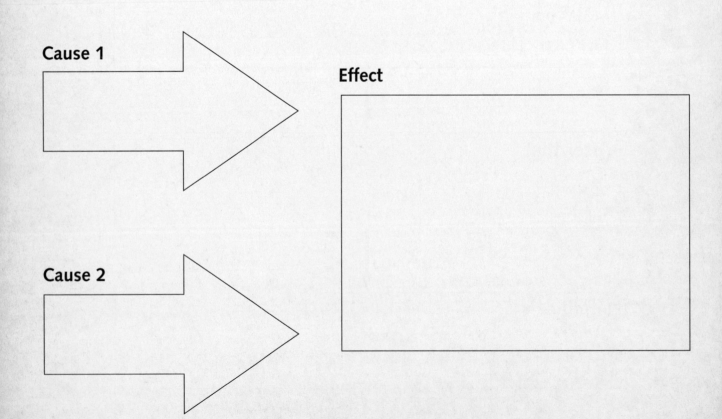

Effect 1

Cause

Effect 2

Cause 1

Effect

Cause 2